The most beautiful people we have known are those who have known defeat, known suffering, known struggle, known loss, and have found their way out of the depths. These persons have an appreciation, a sensitivity and an understanding of life that fills them with compassion, gentleness, and a deep loving concern. Beautiful people do not just happen.

—Elisabeth Kübler-Ross

CONTENTS

WHAT HAPPENED BEFORE

OVER THE PAST 12 years, my family and I have had the honor and privilege to meet many beautiful people. They have paid, perhaps, the highest price there is—the deaths of their children—to acquire their beauty and share it with others. How did they do that? How did they climb out of the depths of their despair to bring so much compassion, deep caring, help and, yes, even joy to so many others? They did not just happen. They got help from other beautiful people on this side of the veil and from their loved ones on the other side. Beautiful people are all around us.

In 2015, I finished writing *Suffering Is the Only Honest Work*, in which I told how we'd lost our son, Jimmy Gauntt, to a freak accident in 2008, and how my father had reached out almost 40 years after his own death to help with healing our grief. For those of you who haven't read *Suffering*, here are the basics of how that book came about.

On December 22, 1970, my father, Grover Gauntt Jr., went to his office, pulled a recently purchased handgun from his briefcase, and died by suicide. Anger and fear overwhelmed me. How could he do that to us? How could the bravest man I knew do that to himself? What would we do now? When the shock wore off, I stuffed the anger deep inside and went on with life, going back to college, wooing Hilary, who would become my wife, getting my law degree, and vowing to forget and never forgive my father for his betrayal.

On August 9, 2008, the medical examiner for San Diego County knocked on our door at first light and gave us the most horrible news parents can receive: Our son, Jimmy, had been struck by a car and killed. He was just three months shy of his 25th birthday. Over the past two years since graduating from USC, Jimmy had been pursuing a professional career in Los Angeles as an actor and writer. Blindly we stumbled through the ensuing days, weeks, and months.

On November eighth, our family went to Del Mar Beach with a zipper-lock bag of Jimmy's ashes. Jimmy's older sister, Brittany, and I paddled out on our boogie boards and watched as Jimmy's remains joined the endless ocean for eternity. Our son-in-law, Ryan, Hilary, and my 87-year-old mother watched us with binoculars from the sand.

Later my mother became tired and I offered to take her home while the others continued to enjoy the gorgeous beach weather. After dropping her off, I swung by our house, checked our mailbox, and found the letter that changed my life forever and started healing the devastation my father had left behind.

The story of "The Letter" became a film by Steve Date, and a chapter in *Suffering*. I won't go into all the details, but long story short, in 1968, fresh out of high school in suburban Chicago, I went to Coalwood, West Virginia, to work on a project with my family's construction company. At the end of that summer, Emily Sue Buck-berry, a woman who had lived in the same boarding house, found a letter my dad wrote to me. She heard I was going home and swung by my room to say goodbye. I had already left, but outside my room, next to a waste basket, she came across the letter. She picked it up and kept it with the intent to one day return it to me. Forty years later she Googled me, called, got my address, and sent the old letter she had recently run across in a box of papers.

My hands trembled as I tore open the priority mail envelope

and for the first time read two full pages in Dad's neat handwriting. His letter was full of fatherly advice and love for me. He spoke of suffering from depression as a youth, the needless death of a younger sister when he was 13, his mother's fanatic religious zeal, and a war that forever changed him.

Then the words that would begin to heal decades of anger and pain, words he had never spoken in life: "I'll be around, any time you want me—I'll be there—because I care more than you'll ever know—my son. All love, Dad."

And their miraculous timing.

You see, November eighth, the day my dad's letter arrived in my hands, was Jimmy's 25th birthday. It arrived on his birthday!

My dad knew that day was going to be one of the hardest days of my life and he was there with me, just as he promised he would be.

I wrote and shared the story of "The Letter" with family and friends, and thus began my transition from a 43-year career as a corporate lawyer to writer. As more synchronicities and "unexplainables" continued to unfold and turn into stories, in 2011 we launched our website, WriteMeSomethingBeautiful.com.

In 2013, a couple of other dads and I started a grief support group in San Diego for fathers who have suffered the death of a child. We call ourselves the Fraternity—the one God forbid you ever have to join.

Our experiences with death and what comes after may not reflect your beliefs, and I honor that. I can speak only of the things my family and I have experienced, and those that others have told us about. We must all come to terms with death according to our spiritual beliefs and customs. However that happens for you, that is your blessing.

This book is about healing. I cannot use the word "healed." As Billy Bob Thornton reflected upon the loss of his younger brother, also a Jimmy, in *O Magazine*, "You won't ever get over it. The more you know it and embrace it, the better off you will be."

But as we progress with our healing we learn to live with our loss, adjust to it, wear it. We learn there are many beautiful, caring and compassionate souls who help us with our healing, whether we know them or not, whether they are still in their bodies or not. Hopefully, at some point, we arrive at a place with our own healing where we can begin to help others with theirs, whether we know them or not, whether still in their bodies or not. We learn we can mend and even forge new relationships with our loved ones beyond their bodies and across several lifetimes.

I wish you comfort, healing, and love.

"I'M CHRISTIAN"

IT WAS MAY of 2016 and I was working as in-house counsel for a large family-owned real estate company in San Diego. I spotted Chris Ramirez in the lobby of the corporate headquarters. Chris ran one of the company's large apartment communities, and we'd become good friends over the last few years. He saw me and came right over. He said, "Casey, you got a minute? There's something I've got to tell you, and it's really important."

We went into the break room, grabbed a cup of coffee, and as soon as we sat down Chris started in. "Casey, my dad died last week." But as he said it, he had this huge grin on his face, and he was aglow.

I thought, "Oh, man. This is going to be good."

After you read Chris's story, "I'm Christian," I think you will agree *good* is a huge understatement.

❦

The only sound Christopher Ramirez heard as he entered the intensive care room was the beep of the monitors and the quiet pulse of the ventilator that kept his father alive. On May 18, 2016, Rogelio Ramirez had suffered a massive stroke that left him paralyzed from the nose down. Only his eyes moved: blink, look up, look down. Rogelio's wife of 56 years, Amelia, sat vigil at his bedside, occasionally relieved by their sons to get some much-needed rest.

The neurologist in charge of Rogelio's case had even worse news for the family. In his office he told them, "Your father suffers from locked-in syndrome, a rare neurological condition. I'm sorry, but there is no cure. He's aware of his surroundings and understands what you say, so be careful when you talk of his condition, which will continue to deteriorate until he dies."

The 79-year-old had been plagued with heart disease and other problems, so at Christopher and his brothers' urging, their parents had moved from Corpus Christi, Texas, to San Diego so the Ramirez boys could take care of them. Now they faced the worst decision children can be asked to make: to pull the plug and let their father die, or keep him alive indefinitely.

The ICU doctors and nurses quickly developed a way to communicate with Rogelio, which they shared with the family. One blink meant "no." Closing his eyes for five seconds meant "yes." This ensured that they could "talk" to him, find out if he was comfortable and, most important, confirm he knew what was happening to him.

The options were extremely limited. "If Mr. Ramirez is left on life support, soon other organs will begin to shut down," the doctor said. "It could be weeks or even months, but he will not survive."

Christopher knew his father wouldn't want to live this way. "He had made this very clear to us a few years ago, after a heart attack," he told the doctor as he, his mother, and two of his brothers spoke with the neurologist.

The doctor replied, "Since Mr. Ramirez can communicate and understand everything that's being said, this will have to be his decision."

Chills ran up and down Christopher's spine as he thought about having to ask his father whether he wanted to remain on the machines keeping him alive or to turn them off and pass peacefully.

The family followed the neurologist into Rogelio's room. The doctor asked, "Mr. Ramirez, do you understand what happened to you?"

Rogelio closed his eyes for five seconds.

"Do you understand that you most likely will not get any better than you are now?"

Again, the eyes closed.

Mrs. Ramirez then asked, "Rogelio, do you want to remain on the machines that are helping you breathe?"

A quick blink at his wife. "No!"

So it was decided. The family made arrangements with the nurses to take him off life support the following morning.

Christopher remembers, "I could not sleep that night. I tossed and turned and finally got up at five and went for a run. I could only think of the decision my father had made, and that within a matter of hours he would no longer be a part of this world. I decided to spend every last minute I could with him."

At 6:15 a.m. Christopher arrived at the hospital, where he found the night nurse giving his father a sponge bath. She wanted him to look his best when the rest of the family arrived. Mrs. Ramirez came in and held her husband's hand for what would be the last time.

Chris's brothers, Carlos and Roger, arrived a short time later. When the nurse came back in the room, they let her know the rest of the family would be there soon.

"Will Christian be coming back?" the nurse asked.

"You must mean Christopher. That's me. I was the first one here."

She gave him a puzzled look. "No, a young man was here before you."

Mrs. Ramirez paled and sank into a chair.

The nurse asked, "Is this someone I should keep away from the ICU?"

Shaking, Christopher answered. "My 10-year-old son passed away four years ago from a blood infection. His name was Christian."

The nurse, shaken, stammered, "Oh, well, all you boys look so much alike. I must have mistaken one of you for someone else." She hurried from the room.

Stunned, the family huddled silently around Rogelio's bed as they waited for the rest of the family to arrive.

After a few minutes, Christopher excused himself and found the night nurse. "Please, tell me what you saw. And how did you come up with the name Christian?"

"I was getting things ready for your father's bath about half an hour before you arrived. I looked up and saw a young man around 15 or 16, who looked a lot like you, standing in the doorway. I asked if I could help him.

"He smiled and said, 'I'm Christian. Would it be okay if I spoke with my grandfather?' I nodded and he came in and sat down. He kissed your dad's forehead and whispered something as I left the room. When I came back a few minutes later, Christian was gone."

Christian would have been 14. His dad took a picture of his nephew Drew, 31, out of his wallet. "Could it have been him?" he asked.

"No. Christian was definitely younger," she replied, becoming agitated. Then she said, "We don't have cameras in patients' rooms, but we do have one that records anyone coming into or out of the ICU. I reviewed the tape a few minutes ago. From five a.m. until just now the only ones who entered were doctors, nurses, and you, your mother and brothers."

"You didn't see Christian on the tape?"

The nurse shook her head. "No."

Christopher rushed back to his father's room before Rogelio was given pain medication that would sedate him and make him comfortable as they removed his ventilation tube and disconnected IVs. By this time the rest of the family had arrived. It was time to say goodbye.

When Christopher's turn came, he said, "Dad, I love you. Don't worry about Mom. We'll all take good care of her. You taught me so much about life and I'm so grateful. I hope I can be as good a father as you were to us."

One question hovered on Christopher's lips. If he didn't ask it, he would regret it forever. With tears trickling down his face, he asked, "Dad, did Christian come see you this morning?"

Tears streamed from Rogelio's eyes as he clenched his eyes shut for five seconds.

Yes.

Rogelio passed away a few hours later, surrounded by family, both in body and in spirit.

*This story is dedicated in loving memory of
Rogelio and Christian Ramirez.*

HEALING ALL AROUND

IN 2017, JIMMY'S good friend John Schuyler asked me to be best man in his and Samantha's wedding. We've known John and his family since he was in diapers. We are as close to family as you can get. When he came over to the house to ask me, he said, "Jimmy was like a brother to me and I always thought he would be my best man. Since that can't be, I'd like you to stand in."

I was humbled and of course I said yes. But I cautioned, "This sends a loud message and Jimmy will be front and center in everyone's minds at the wedding. Are you sure you and Sam are okay with that?"

His reply was firm. "That's why I'm asking you." This was a big leap for someone who until two years before could barely speak Jimmy's name in our presence.

I struggled for months over what to say—or not to say—in my Best Man toast. I'm very comfortable speaking before large audiences, but this was different. This was a very big deal. I frequently huddled with Hilary, Brittany, and Ryan to share thoughts. What would Jimmy have said if he'd been here? What would he want me to say?

One week before the wedding, Hilary was cleaning out an old

file cabinet she hadn't touched in 15 years. It was crammed with newspaper clippings, school papers, report cards, and other memorabilia of when Brittany and Jimmy were kids. Hilary dreaded going into that rabbit hole. For her it was like Superman's kryptonite. Peeling back all of those memories of Jimmy was just too much for her. But she got a nudge—more of a shove, really—and a clear message from Jimmy to "suck it up and get in there!"

In the middle of her "archeological dig" she stumbled upon a letter. It was a full page, typed. The signature at the bottom: *Jimmy Gauntt*. He had written it in the spring of 2001 in support of John's application to Brown University. He had written everything we'd been thinking of, and he wrote it so much better than we ever could. We could almost hear him laughing: "Here you go. Just read this, Dad."

And, of course, John got into Brown.

The wedding was on Friday, September 22nd—what would have been my father's 98th birthday—at the historic Avalon Hotel in old Palm Springs. We got there on Thursday for golf with the groomsmen and the rehearsal dinner that night at Spencer's, a very fine restaurant at a tennis club tucked up against the mountains.

When it was time to toast the newlyweds, I stood and introduced myself, then began to speak. "My wife and I have known John since he was two years old and have an enormous well of information about him." Winking at John, I said, "That isn't necessarily a good thing for you, my friend." When the laughter died down, I continued.

"I am so honored and humbled to be your best man, even though I was not your first choice. I am proud to stand for you on behalf of our son and your good pal, Jimmy Gauntt, and our family. Jimmy's big sister, Brittany Kirby, would like to read from the letter Jimmy wrote for you back in 2001. Thank you, Jimmy, for coming to our rescue and showing up to perform your duties as John's first choice."

Brittany rose, cleared her throat, and began reading the words

Jimmy had written so long ago, a testament to John's character and to Jimmy's as well. "In all the years I've known John, I've come to see him not just as a friend but as a big brother," Jimmy had written. He told how John, even though he was a year ahead of Jimmy, made sure he was picked for the flag football team at recess and stood up for him when a bigger kid picked on him.

She went on to read Jimmy's praise of his friend. "John is always willing to hear new ideas and opinions, but he is also never reluctant to have his own voice be heard." Jimmy admired John's ability to make people laugh, as well as his leadership skills. "Even though John was the best player on the football team, he never bragged; he let his actions speak for him. While most guys talk about how great they are, John proves it by trying his hardest in everything he does."

The character reference ended with these words: "John has helped me in so many ways, receiving nothing in return other than my thanks and friendship… I'm lucky to have John as a big brother. As long as John is my friend, I know I will never be alone."

Brittany sat, and I went on with the toast. "John, you and Jimmy will always be brothers. The Schuylers are family to us. Samantha, today you have officially become a member of the Schuyler family, and that also makes you a member of the Gauntt-Kirby family. We welcome you with wide-open arms and loving hearts. Let's raise our glasses to Sam and John. May your lifetimes, and then some, be filled with joy, happiness, vibrant health and, above all, love."

Brittany and I got through the toast without breaking down. Misty eyes and choked sobs came from the rest of the crowd.

This was only the second wedding of Jimmy's friends we had attended. The first one had been more of a spectacle: New Year's Eve, three bands, a price tag you could hang on a star. We couldn't help but wonder: Would our son be married now? What would he be doing? Following his passion for writing?

Nine years later and it was still hard for Hilary to see Jimmy's friends married, some with kids, well into their careers. Yet tonight she hugged everybody, wore her beautiful smile and party shoes, and soldiered on, setting a shining example of grace for us and all of Jimmy's friends who missed their pal. They've been suffering mightily, too, and haven't stopped asking themselves, "Why him?" I could feel the healing taking place.

After the toasts some people went to the dance floor. Others, including me, chose the bar. As I sipped my cocktail, a young, tall, good-looking man came up to me. Looking me in the eye seemed to be a chore for him. He stood ramrod straight as he said, "Mr. Gauntt, your toast touched me deeply on multiple levels. I'm Henry Armstrong."

The name was familiar but I didn't know why. We shook hands and, as I was still trying to place the name, Hilary walked up. I said, "Hilary, this is Henry Armstrong."

Hilary's eyes widened, tears ready to fall. "*The* Henry Armstrong? Can I give you a hug?" He nodded and they held on to each other like their lives depended on it.

Henry had been the last person to see Jimmy alive. The two had gone bar hopping with other friends from high school. After a night of hard partying, Henry and Jimmy took a taxi back to Henry's house in nearby Rancho Santa Fe to continue the fun. Finally, Mrs. Armstrong made them go to bed around three a.m. in separate rooms. Just before first light, Jimmy got up and decided to make the five-mile walk home. He didn't make it.

After the accident, suffocated by our own pain, we never reached out to Henry or heard from him. We reached out to the driver of the car that struck Jimmy, but not Henry. We couldn't face hearing the details of those final moments from the last person to see him. Dealing with our own nightmares blotted out everything, including all the struggles Henry must have been going through.

Hilary and I spoke with Henry, happy to hear what he'd been doing. He told us he had graduated from law school in 2008 and had taken the California Bar exam just two weeks before Jimmy's accident. For the past nine years he'd been with the Los Angeles office of a prestigious New York law firm.

I gave him a bear hug, we both cried, and I put my hand on his heart. "I know I am meant to be here in Palm Springs hugging and talking to you at this moment. I believe Jimmy orchestrated this whole evening. He has a habit of doing stuff like this."

By now Brittany had joined us and Hilary took Henry's arm. "It's too noisy in here. Let's go someplace quiet and talk." She and Britt led Henry away, leaving me to contemplate this extremely unexpected turn of events. I had thought we were here for one reason, so I could stand in for Jimmy and toast his buddy, John. And that certainly was one reason, but Jimmy all along had a deeper, more powerful purpose. We were here to help Henry heal.

I saw Henry when he came back to the party. He seemed lighter and less anxious.

Later, Hilary and Brittany told me how devastated and guilty he had felt for all these years. Why was he the last guy with Jimmy? What could he have done differently to maybe prevent Jimmy from leaving his house? Why couldn't he reach out to us? Of course, the women assured him it was nobody's fault but Jimmy's. Jimmy was buzzed, never had any sense of direction (just like his old man), and decided to walk home—going the wrong way—on a dark, winding, narrow road with no shoulders or sidewalks.

As Hilary and I checked out on Saturday morning, the last person we saw before getting into the car was Henry Armstrong. One more hug before we hit the road.

Big healing all around.

Please note some of the characters' names have been modified in respect for their privacy.

FRIENDS: THE FORGOTTEN ONES

WE LEARNED SOME valuable lessons at John Schuyler's wedding. Only a handful of Jimmy's friends stayed close to us in the months and years after Jimmy's accident. Most—including some of his closest friends— did not. It wasn't because they didn't want to. It wasn't because they had moved on, put him in their minds' dark closets. They didn't know how to approach us, and we didn't give them permission.

We learned that they, too, were suffering mightily and yet were reluctant to reach out to us to share a memory, a photo, their pain, for fear that would only add to our suffering. They felt guilty as their lives went on—new jobs, getting married, having kids—but their pal was stuck at 24. They weren't neglecting us. They were protecting us.

We as the parents didn't do a very good job of lessening this guilt. We were invited but didn't—couldn't—go to weddings of Jimmy's friends those first years. We'd been to family weddings; we felt safe at those. And we sort of had to go to John's because he asked me to be best man.

Because it was so hard for us to be with Jimmy's friends and celebrate them moving forward—like watching the mother-son dance that Hilary will never have—we unintentionally sent them a message: *Your lives have gone on. Jimmy's hasn't. Stay away. Leave us alone.* We pushed his friends away. We didn't mean to, but we did.

That is why so many of Jimmy's friends mobbed us at John's wedding. By showing up, standing in place of Jimmy as John's best man, and sharing so much of Jimmy in my toast, we unlocked the door. We declared loud and clear, "Jimmy is in the house!" We gave them permission to talk with us about Jimmy. And, boy, did they jump through that open door. Henry was first, followed by a steady stream.

They told us how much they missed Jimmy and how having us there brought Jimmy closer to them. They shared stories of him, messages from him, laughs, tears, misgivings, guilt from that last night, remorse, and just plain grief. Jimmy's presence was palpable.

We were a critical conduit for them to unburden themselves with the pain and pent-up feelings they'd been lugging around the past nine years. We helped them with their healing.

We parents of those whose lives have been cut way too short have an important role to play—dare I say an obligation—to help our children's friends with their healing. We had forgotten that they lost him, too.

Don't wait for them to reach out. They won't. They are scared to death of picking at that scab of grief (they may think that's what will happen, but it doesn't—quite the opposite), so they just leave us alone. They suffer in silence with nowhere to go to express their grief, and we parents assume they've moved on.

We hold the keys to grief's doors that only we can open and let others pass through. The friends so want and need to talk to us and feel connected to the one they lost, too.

Invite them in. Open the door. Give them permission to grieve with you. Send them a note. *Hi, Nik, I've been thinking about you...*

If you see them at a store, say something like "I just ran into one of Jimmy's friends from elementary school…" It can be as simple as saying Jimmy's name. That's a door opener.

Helping Jimmy's friends heal has helped us heal. By unlocking the door and giving them permission to enter, we've removed that awkwardness of the unsaid as the elephant hovers nearby.

GREETING GRIEF

SOON AFTER WE put up "How to Write a Beautiful Condolence Card to Someone Who Has Lost a Child" on our website, I sent the link to our good friend and fellow James Taylor aficionado, Diane, and thanked her, again, for writing us such a wonderful letter after our son Jimmy died. I received a letter from Diane a week later.

When her father died in 1988, she was 33 and had never before experienced hard loss. Following that devastating event, she put together several do's and don'ts on how to interact with friends and acquaintances who have suffered a loss of someone they deeply love. They are definitely worth sharing.

She wrote, "It is always present in our souls because our loved one is always on our minds. Others around us are usually afraid to mention it for fear it will stir up a sad emotion. However, I discovered that it is the opposite. If a person mentions their name or asks me how I'm doing, it actually brings me comfort because I realize that someone else is acknowledging my grief."

When we received the news of Jimmy's death on that August morning, I literally felt something hit my side and shove me onto a different playing field where the previous rules of engagement for how people would interact with us, and we with them, suddenly all changed. We were the gravely wounded, trying to navigate a new world.

This gigantic wave of pain and suffering also hit other family members, Jimmy's wide circle of friends, our friends, and all those people who touched Jimmy's and our lives over the years. Thousands of people. The wave hit people we didn't even know, but who were nonetheless deeply impacted, because our son's death triggered their grief for loved ones lost. I think reverberation is the word for that.

We were also disoriented by a number of friends who simply weren't there, who were afraid or too busy or simply didn't know what to say or do.

I get that. Over a decade has passed since Jimmy made his transition, and one of my cousins, someone I thought I was close to, has never said or written anything to me about the loss of our son. Several months after Jimmy died, I stumbled upon a photograph of my cousin's youngest sister taken a few months before she was killed in a horse jumping accident at the age of 12. I sent it to him in the pathetic hope he might contact me. Surely he would appreciate the thought and would reach out to me and we would talk about Jimmy, and his sister. Nope. Nothing.

Hilary dreaded going to the local grocery store for weeks and months after Jimmy left us. She would always see someone she knew and, too often, the person would turn her cart into another aisle or flee the store so she wouldn't have to talk about "it." This hurt Hilary deeply and also made her angry. As she tearfully described one such encounter, she exclaimed, "I hate being treated as a victim!" She found another grocery store outside the neighborhood.

I'm guilty of the same offense. Four months before we lost Jimmy, the middle son of some friends of ours died of an accidental drug overdose. Shortly after his death I saw Gary, his father, at a golf tournament. I spun around and hightailed it the other way so I wouldn't have to talk to him.

Two months later Gary and his wife, Kay, came to Jimmy's

memorial service. Within seconds Gary and I were in a bear hug, tears flowing as we mourned the loss of our boys.

A couple of months after the service, Hilary and I had dinner with two of our closest friends from college. We talked about their kids, a boy and girl almost identical in ages to ours, trips they had planned, everything except Jimmy. Not once in the two hours we were together did they ever mention Jimmy or ask how we were doing. Had they forgotten Jimmy? Thought he no longer existed, even in memory?

This is juxtaposed with our good friends Penny and Frank Schuyler, who invited us for dinner every Saturday night for over a year. They always encouraged us to talk about Jimmy and relive our favorite memories of him. Mostly they listened—and sometimes squirmed—about the many ways we approached our grief, including our experiences with mediums, shamans, and Indian guides.

Very early on, when our grief was so raw and painful, Hilary's aunt and uncle, Kathy and Brud, flew from Florida for no other reason than to have lunch with us. They had walked through our valley 27 years earlier, when their 22-year old son died.

At one point, Hilary asked, "Do you ever stop thinking about your son? That he died? Does the pain ever go away?"

Uncle Brud, once one of the finest heart surgeons in the country, had spent his career on the edge of life and death. Tears streaked his cheeks as he took Hilary's hands. His cultured Southern drawl washed over us. "Oh, darlin,' you never forget. You don't want to forget. You will always love 'em and they will always love you."

When you are with or see someone who has lost a child, it is important to keep in mind that in those first few days, months, and even years, the elephant is always in the room with them. The parents' pain, heartache, and shock might as well be a deep gash down the middle of their faces. It's hard, but don't look away. Don't pretend it isn't there or act like it didn't happen. I've been on both sides of that fence and I'm ashamed of how badly I handled my encounters before Jimmy died.

I walked into the gym I'd belonged to for ten years for the first time in the three weeks since his death. My thoughts were still fogged, but I needed to stay in shape. It might be the only thing that would keep me sane. Nervousness roiled my stomach. As I looked around, I wondered who knew. Did everyone know Jimmy died? Why would they?

Tony, a fellow gym rat I knew casually, walked toward me. I wondered if he knew. As he said, "Hi, how's it going?" he seemed tight. Maybe he did know.

My thoughts kicked in. *Should I say something? No. That will make Tony uncomfortable. I don't want to drag him into my nightmare.*

Much later, Tony told me his first thought was *Oh, shit, there's Casey. His son died. Young guy, too. He must be close to out of his mind. How can he possibly get through this? I couldn't do it.*

His next thought was *I'll suck it up, say hi, but I won't mention his son. Casey doesn't want to talk about him. That will make him feel worse.* Then we each headed off to do our thing.

Tony made the wrong call as he tried to spare my feelings that day. Why wouldn't I want to talk about Jimmy when that was the only thing I could think of? My mind was entirely taken over by his death. It was like a bad song stuck on repeat. No, it was worse than that. Much worse.

I could tell Tony knew about Jimmy's death. I was more than just hurt. Didn't he know how horrible I was feeling? I, too, felt so much the victim. Was death all that Tony could see around me? Did I die along with my son in the eyes of my friends?

I did, a bit. Part of me died. Maybe I had a new name: Casey-who-lost-his-son Gauntt. Were my elephant and I not welcome anymore? Crazy thoughts? Not really.

Yes, Tony should have said something. But that's when I made my second mistake. I didn't bring it up. I should have said, "Tony,

I don't know if you heard, but I lost my son three weeks ago." I assumed Tony didn't want to talk about it. Now I realize he simply didn't know how.

When Hilary and I had dinner with our friends, rather than crawling into our dark place and waiting, we should have said something like "We were looking at some photos of our trip to Sun Valley with you guys when Jimmy and Greg were five. Remember how excited they were when they hooked their first fish?"

We are victims, but that doesn't mean we have to act like victims.

Tony and I learned some valuable lessons that day. In the age of the internet, ubiquitous mobile devices, and our insatiable hunger for gossip, the news of Jimmy's death traveled fast and wide, and virtually everyone who knew me, even casually, knew what happened to Jimmy within 48 hours. When I walked into the gym that day, I would venture a guess that almost everybody knew what had happened. My first mistake was to assume otherwise.

After these early stumbles and uncomfortable encounters, I learned pretty fast that when I was with someone—a colleague, a client, a friend—if they didn't bring up Jimmy early in the conversation, I should. I met them halfway. And they were always—always!—so relieved and appreciative that I did. Once that door opened, they dove right through in a wave of pent-up emotion and sympathy. They were not only grateful I had opened the door, they were often eager to talk. About Jimmy. And often about the loss of someone close to them. I gave them permission to mourn and grieve with me.

I've come a long way. Recently I visited my dentist to get my teeth cleaned. I had not met Debbie, the new hygienist, before. She was friendly and made light "getting to know me" conversation. She asked, "Are you married?"

"Yes." I knew exactly what her next question would be. "So, tell me, Casey, do you have kids?"

I told her about Brittany, Ryan, and their two boys, and that they live close to us.

"Oh, that's nice they're near you," Debbie chirped.

"And we have a son, Jimmy. He was accidentally struck and killed by an automobile walking home from a friend's house almost 12 years ago."

She graciously expressed her shock and sympathies. And then she launched into a story of her older sister who had died almost two years ago after a long battle with cancer. "My sister visits me in my dreams. They are so vivid and real. I've been having some problems with my youngest daughter in high school. My sister came to me in a dream last week and gave me the perfect advice for how to help her niece."

I briefly mentioned the many ways Jimmy has stayed connected with us.

There was electricity in the room as she exclaimed, "I've got goose bumps!"

I observed, "Do you see what just happened? I could have said, 'We have a daughter' and left it at that. But I shared with you our big truth because it felt right. We deeply connected. It's so easy, but we avoid what we think are 'uncomfortable' conversations when, in fact, they are anything but."

Debbie said, "This is the best conversation I've ever had with a patient, and I've been doing this for over 20 years."

We exchanged email addresses so I could send her some of our stories. Never before had I hugged a hygienist.

Everyone has lost someone close, or soon will. Death, loss, and grief are all around us, creating profound impacts on our lives and opportunities to deeply connect with others, and yet it seems most just can't talk about it. Guys are the worst. Why is that? Are we afraid we will seem weak if we don't buck up, soldier on, put it all behind us and get on with life? Let me tell you something. The strongest guys I know are those who can and will talk about it. It takes real guts to open to the sorrow.

Other than Tony's lame "How's it going?" no one else spoke to me that first day back at the gym. As I was leaving, I ran into Danny Davis, a former Navy SEAL and my trainer for many years. He looked at me and he, too, didn't say anything. Instead he approached with arms outstretched, wrapping me tightly in his friendship. I burst into tears.

After a minute or so he said, "Are you hungry? Let's go grab a sandwich."

As we ate, we talked for over an hour about Jimmy. And still do. Danny Davis is one of the strongest guys I know.

Postscript: Remember our good friends who never mentioned Jimmy during our dinner with them? The Monday following that dinner I got the call from Emily Sue Buckberry, and a few days later the letter from my father arrived in my mailbox. A month after that we had dinner once again with our friends, again in the same restaurant. I told them the story of the letter from my father, and the emotional dam broke. For the rest of the evening, we all cried and talked about our best memories of Jimmy.

They bemoaned our previous get-together. "We didn't know what to do. It hurt us, too, not to mention him. Thank you for showing us it's okay to talk about that boy we love so much."

It's much better than okay. It's essential.

All you have to do sometimes is open the door.

HEALING WITH HISTORY

WHEN WE SUFFER a devastating loss, we think it's unique, that no one has suffered more than we have. After a while, when the shock subsides, we're willing to look further. After Jimmy's death, it took some time, but when I began researching my family, going back several generations, I found that heartache is universal. And in a way I found some peace with that.

After I received my father's letter that Emily Sue Buckberry had safeguarded for 40 years, I knew I needed to find out more about him. I had to probe the things he revealed to me: his childhood depression, his fanatical, religious mother he couldn't reason with, and a war that he wouldn't talk about. What happened to him? Why didn't he think he was successful? Why did he end his life? So many questions. But I wasn't ready to delve into those—not even close. I'd spent the last 38 years doing my best to forget him, running away hard from his memory. I was like an aircraft carrier in full retreat. It's not that easy to change course.

So, instead I wrote about my grandfather, Vernon Drury Case, the man I was named after and the man who, next to my dad and Jimmy, had the biggest influence on my life.

Vern Case was one of those bigger-than-life guys. He was born in 1897 and grew up in Willits, about 100 miles north of San Francisco. The Case clan was among the early settlers of this small logging and farming town in Mendocino County. Vern's grandparents came to California from Missouri by wagon train in 1854. After a couple of lean years scratching for gold at the Rough and Ready mining camp on the western slopes of the Sierras, they pulled up stakes and headed for Willits.

Like most boys his age, Vern started working on the family farm at age six and attended a one-room schoolhouse with one overworked teacher for all of grades one through eight. Vern's father, Drury, was a slavedriver. Vern didn't mind the hard work, but he despised his father's foul temper, fueled by Dru's struggles with alcoholism, and the beatings his old man's whip delivered to him and his three brothers. He also hated being poor and wearing his brothers' hand-me-downs.

Vern refused to attend his father's funeral in 1939 and rarely spoke of him. However, he inherited his father's six-foot four-inch height and his extraordinary work ethic. Vern left school after the seventh grade and went to work for a logging company. He moved out of the house at 14 and, driven by his relentless desire to succeed, embarked on a career nothing short of extraordinary.

By the early 1940s, Vern and his partner, W.A. Johnson, had their own company, performing construction work all over the country for the Department of Defense during World War II. One of their biggest projects was dredging San Diego Bay to permit deep-draft warships to enter the protected harbor. Vern and his family lived in the Hotel Del Coronado for two years while he oversaw that job. He traveled extensively to Washington, D.C. to lobby generals, admirals, and elected officials for more work.

In 1953, Vern and his wife and partner, Henrietta, moved to Chicago and launched Case Foundation Company. Over the next 20 years, Case became one of the most successful deep-foundation construction companies in the United States, with offices in Panama,

Puerto Rico, and Brazil. Case Foundation will forever be identified with a significant portion of Chicago's skyline, having installed the drilled shaft foundations for many of the city's dominant skyscrapers, including Marina City, Cabrini Towers, Trump Tower, and the 100-plus-story behemoths: Sears Tower, the Standard Oil Building, and John Hancock Tower.

I was in awe of this man who emerged from abject poverty, hauled logs down the slopes of the Sierras by mule-drawn wagons, and progressed to riding to job sites in chauffeur-driven limousines, all within a span of 50 years. I took great pleasure digging into Vern's life with my mother, Barbara, and her brother, my uncle Stan.

I also found it very healing to delve deeper into my roots, retrace the steps of my ancestors back to Scotland and England, and look across generations of my clan. It had only been ten months since Jimmy's death, but as I was pulling Vern's story together, I began to feel more grounded. It was as though an anchor spilled out of my rudderless ship that floundered in a turbulent sea of profound grief. The storm had not calmed, but I was no longer helpless against the surging sorrow. It was also good practice for the heavy lifting that was looming before me with my father.

"My thought process has been prejudiced by a depression in my youth and insecurity, by a religious fanatical mother who I could not reason with, by a war in which I was in the infantry, and so forth." My father wrote those words in the letter he tried to send to me in Coalwood.

I wrote this in the introduction to the chapter "My Father" in *Suffering Is the Only Honest Work*: "Though life seems to be lived linearly, we gather information sporadically, sometimes not becoming privy to relevant knowledge until well after events that seem inexplicable when they happen. If I had known more about my father's past, I might have been less appalled and more empathetic when he died. As it was, I discovered far too late the influences that shaped the man who meant more to me than anyone except Jimmy."

If I were to write that intro today, I would delete *far too late*. It's never too late, as you will find out as you read on.

I extensively interrogated Stan and my mother to learn everything I could about my father, his ancestors, his childhood, his service in World War II, and his post-war career working for his father-in-law's company, Case Foundation. As Jimmy had done before me, I read the numerous letters my father wrote to his parents and his girlfriend, Barbara, during the war. I researched the battles he and his fellow soldiers fought in the South Pacific. I spoke with some of the guys he worked with at Case. I sat down with my brother and sister.

I first shared "Grover Cleveland Gauntt, Jr.—The Early Years (1919–1946)" with my immediate family and then cousins and friends. For the first time in a long time, our extended family began to talk about him. We shone light on the man and his story, and illuminated the darkness surrounding his suicide. Here are some of the things I learned about my dad.

The Gauntt clan emigrated from Lincolnshire, England, in the 1660s and settled in Plymouth, Massachusetts. From there they migrated into the Carolinas and then to Texas in the 1850s.

Grover Jr. was born in 1919 in Fort Worth, Texas. A few years later his father, a seller of women's clothing, moved the family to Glendale, California.

In 1932 Dad's younger sister, Anna Louise, died of diphtheria at age six. The vaccine that could have saved her was shunned by her Christian Science parents. Her needless death made a huge impression on a 13-year-old boy. As penance, his mother joined an obscure religious cult, removed all photographs from their house, and spent most weekends attending services, away from their home and her other three children. Her husband spent more and more time working in his women's clothing store and traveling to the east, ostensibly to purchase the latest fashions.

Grover Jr. was a student leader and graduated with honors from

Glendale High School and UCLA, where his oldest sister, Imogene, was the first homecoming queen. He met Barbara Case when he was a senior and she a sophomore at the University of Southern California.

Immediately upon graduation in 1941, he joined the U.S. Army as a second lieutenant. Six months later, Japan attacked Pearl Harbor. After two years of training in California, Captain Gauntt and the 145th Infantry Regiment shipped out to the Pacific Theater.

After a year of bloody fighting in the Solomon Islands, my father, now 25, became the youngest person to achieve the rank of major in the Pacific Theater. He was part of the Army's 37th Division that invaded the Philippines. By the war's end in September of 1945, Major Gauntt was an intelligence officer and battalion commander in charge of over 600 soldiers.

During those two years, my father saw too much death and the horrific things man can inflict upon his fellow man. As Commander of the 1st Battalion, he made decisions that protected his men and also led them to their deaths. Of the 5,000 men of the 145th Infantry Regiment that left San Francisco harbor in January of 1944, over half were either killed or wounded. Many more came back with injuries that could not be seen. Major Gauntt was one of those. Even his two Bronze Stars and the Legion of Merit couldn't heal his soul-deep wounds.

Six weeks after returning to California, Grover Jr. and Barbara were married in Los Angeles, affirming life after so much death.

My mother's early life came to light when I asked her to jot down some notes. She sent 20 pages chockful of facts and anecdotes. Barb had proudly served as a first lieutenant in the Army, working for a Washington, D.C. intelligence agency, giving her and my father one more thing in common.

My mother was a packrat when it came to family history and memories. In her archives were every one of my report cards from grade school through college and clippings of every article in which any of her children's names appeared. Perhaps most treasured were all of the writings of her mother, Henrietta Ellis Case.

Henrietta, or Nana to us grandkids, was born in Glenville, California in 1897, the last of 11 children. Tragically, a diphtheria epidemic claimed her two oldest brothers. Henrietta was the first in her family to graduate from college, earning a degree in teaching from Fresno Normal Teachers College (now Fresno State). She taught grade school in Porterville and Oakland for a few years before she married Vern on Valentine's Day in 1920.

Nana was wicked smart, and Vern never hesitated to tip his hat to her for his success in building and managing their businesses. She was also a prolific writer, producing reams of journals, short stories, and poems. I suppose it was Nana's diligence in writing down stories about our ancestors that got me interested in our family's history. And why I was shocked when I stumbled upon an incredible story of courage and survival of one of our ancestors.

In the spring of 2018, I had recently retired and was building out our family tree on Ancestry.com. I was looking for basic facts—date and place of birth, death, and so forth—for my third great-aunt, Mary Sawyers. Mary's older sister, Melcena, was Vern's grandmother. I ran across one of Ancestry's "Hints," a one-paragraph blurb posted by another relative, that Mary and her 18-month-old daughter were among the survivors of the sinking of the SS *Central America* in the Caribbean in 1857. Mary was only 18. Her husband, Sam Swan, and 436 men, including the captain of the ship, perished.

I was stunned. I had never heard one word about this. I checked with other family members and they, too, were clueless. This was the worst peacetime disaster in American maritime history and the tragedy was covered extensively by the papers on both coasts. I began in earnest to search for more of Mary's story.

Mary was born in Missouri in 1839. Her mother died when she was four, and her two older brothers died of cholera six years later. In 1854, 15-year-old Mary and the remnants of her family, lured by stories of gold, joined a wagon train heading to California. Indians attacked as they crossed the Nebraska Territory, and Melcena was seriously wounded.

At 16, Mary and Sam were married at the Rough and Ready camp. A month later, Mary gave birth to their daughter, Lizzie.

Unlike Mary's folks, Sam had some luck finding gold, and in 1857 he decided to return to his home in Pennsylvania with his young family. They took a steamship from San Francisco to the west coast of Panama and crossed the isthmus by railroad. They boarded the SS *Central America*, a sidewheel steamboat, and made their way across the Caribbean bound for New York City. Off Cuba a breeze became a hurricane and disabled the ship. After four days of passengers and crew manning handpumps in a desperate attempt to keep the ship afloat, Captain Herndon ordered women and children to the lifeboats, where they were picked up by the brig *Marine*. The *Central America* sank a few hours later.

Before the ship went down, Herndon gave Mary his gold watch with instructions to give it to his wife and daughter in Albany, New York. A week later, the rescued passengers limped into New York City and Mary fulfilled the captain's last wish. At the time, Herndon's daughter, Ellen, was engaged to a young lawyer, Chester Arthur. Arthur would later become the 21st President of the United States, and Chester and Mary remained lifelong friends and correspondents. But there was more.

After their rescue, Mary elected to stay on the East Coast and moved in with some of Sam's relatives in Pennsylvania. She joined the Union Army and nursed the wounded during the Civil War, amassing considerable medical training at the bloody field hospitals in Pennsylvania.

She later remarried and had seven more children with George Cook. In 1875, Mary and Sam's daughter, Lizzie, who was engaged to be married, was killed in a horseback riding accident at the age of 19. Mary and her new family returned to California the following year and she was reunited with her family in Willits. It had been 20 years since they had last seen one another at the Rough and Ready.

More catastrophes lay ahead. In 1901, George burned to death in the great fire that destroyed most of Willits, including their house. Mary's new house was damaged by the 1906 devasting earthquake that leveled much of San Francisco. After that, Mary lived out her remaining years in relative peace, serving as the town's de facto doctor, surrounded by her kids, 12 grandchildren, and five great-grandchildren. She died in 1924 at the age of 85.

I've found healing and perspective in writing and sharing these stories of my family and ancestors. I realized I'm not the only one to have suffered the loss of a child or ire with a parent. Far from it. Every one of the generations that preceded mine suffered mightily and lived hard lives. No one was spared or got a pass. I took some strange comfort from the fact that I hadn't been singled out for the tragedies I'd been dealt. As I did this work, I also felt surrounded, supported, and loved. Sharing these stories brought me closer to my brother and sister, my cousins and extended family. In a strange way, I also felt the love of my subjects who had left their bodies. Perhaps none greater than Mary's and my dad's.

There was something different, a bit strange, about Mary's story. With the others, I felt I was in charge and doing most of the work, with help, of course, from family members. However, from the moment I fell into Mary's story, and as I uncovered nugget after nugget, I could not shake the feeling Mary wanted her story to be told, and that she had tapped me to do it. She seemingly lit the path for me to follow, easily opening doors at the Library of Congress and other university libraries to help chase down her story.

After three months of researching and writing, I posted Mary's story on our website. GenealogyBank.com picked it up and ran it in three parts on their blog, and I presented her story at the annual meeting of the North San Diego County Genealogy Society. I also pitched her story to film and TV producers, so far to no avail.

After spending so much time with Mary, I felt a bond with her. Because her story was so well preserved by extensive interviews she gave to newspapers over the years, I know her. If I bumped into Mary on the street tomorrow, I have no doubt we'd recognize each other, share a big hug, and sit down and have one fascinating conversation.

I don't think of her as dead. She feels very close and present.

As for my dad, I'll be getting back to him a little later.

And it turns out Ancestry.com had an even bigger surprise in store for our family.

∽

If you would like to read the full stories mentioned in this chapter, together with lots of photos, they can be found on our website by searching www.writemesomethingbeautiful.com/

VERN CASE
GROVER C. GAUNTT, JR
BARBARA CASE GAUNTT
MARY SAWYERS SWAN COOK

MOTHER AND CHILD REUNION

NOT ALL REUNIONS between parent and child take place on the spiritual plane. Hilary and I found that out a couple of years ago when we joined Ancestry.com. Our Christmas gifts to each other were the DNA test. Just for the heck of it, we also gave one to Hilary's mother, Virginia, for her 90th birthday.

I was not shocked to learn I am all WASP—White Anglo-Saxon Protestant—with 86 percent of my forebears coming from England, Scotland, and Wales, and the rest from Scandinavia and Iceland. Maybe that Viking warrior DNA helped me in my career as a lawyer, and it sure has made me strong enough to tackle all the events that have occurred since Jimmy made his transition.

Hilary, on the other hand, was surprised to find out she is 62 percent Scots-English blended in with Irish, German, and Czech roots.

I'm the contact person for the DNA hits, and we've received several expected matches with first through sixth cousins who have also taken the test. There have also been a couple of "whoas"!

In September of 2018, I got an Ancestry.com message from a Cara in Texas, who wrote: *Hi Vernon* [I go by my real name, Vernon Case Gauntt]. *I just wanted to extend an unexpected, sincere thank-you! I am adopted and met my biological paternal grandmother yesterday.*

I don't think this would have happened if your DNA had not come up with a match with me. That, together with all the work you have done on your family tree, led me to my biological father's mother, Linda McDonald. Armed with this information, I had enough confidence to reach out to her and she accepted my invitation to get together. Thank you for unknowingly providing me such an important connection!

Linda is my second cousin and descends from the Gauntt clan, and I was able to share more stories and photos of our ancestors with Cara.

However, that connection didn't come close to the Richter Scale-worthy seismic event that struck six months later. Two days changed many lives forever.

On a Tuesday morning in March, I dropped off Hilary at Lindbergh Field in San Diego. She was headed for Cabo San Lucas with her mahjong group for a few days of intense competition. We must have been running late, because I didn't check my email before leaving for the airport.

When I came home, I got on my laptop and scrolled through new messages. One from Ancestry.com had been sent late Monday night. I opened it immediately.

A MESSAGE FROM JEFFSET:

Hello Vernon, my name is Jeff Pehrson. I was born in February of 1967 in San Francisco. I was then given up for adoption. My adoption was handled through The Children's Home Society. I was adopted by the Pehrson family in May of 1967. I recently did my Ancestry test and HG and I matched as "close family." I know next to nothing about my natural parents, or any natural family. I'd love to learn anything I possibly can. If you'd be so good as to get back to me, I'd sure appreciate it. Thanks so much, Jeff

Oh, my God! HG: Hilary Gauntt. *Did Hilary have a baby she never told me about?* In February of 1967 she was 16 years old, so a secret baby was not impossible but highly unlikely.

I clicked the VIEW THE MATCH link and scanned the results: *Indication is Jeff could be Hilary's first cousin.* So no child hidden in her past. Still…

And then this bombshell: *This also appears to indicate Jeff shares a strong match with Virginia Tedrow—possibly Parent/Child.*

Wait a minute! How could a 39-year-old Virginia have hidden a pregnancy from her husband and three daughters? Not impossible, but again, unlikely.

Then I remembered something Hilary mentioned many years ago. I called her, but no answer. Already in the air. Damn!

I sent her a text and begged her to call me as soon as she landed in Cabo. I also emailed her Jeff's message and the DNA results.

A couple of hours later, Hilary called and her excitement nearly blew out my eardrum. "Oh, my God! This has to be Ainsley's son. The date, the Children's Home Society that our mother volunteered at in Chicago and San Francisco—there's no question Jeff is Ainsley's son!"

Ainsley is Hilary's older sister by two years. In 1967 she was 18, a recent grad of Menlo Atherton High School. Hilary had told me early in our courtship that Ainsley had had a baby right out of high school.

Hilary asked—more like demanded— "What are you going to do?"

Me? This seemed to be a Tedrow issue, not a Gauntt. Still, I wanted to be supportive. "When you come home, we can figure this out."

Hilary wasn't having any of my delaying tactics. "You need to deal with this, now!" she insisted.

And she-who-is-always-right was. I sent Ainsley a carefully worded text—the fact that I was texting her at all surely sent up warning flares: *Hi, Ains. Give me a call when you get a chance. I have some interesting news to share with you.* Lame, I know, but that's the best I could think of.

While I waited to hear back from Ainsley, I brought Brittany into the loop.

Ainsley called a couple of hours later. She has lived in the Bay Area all her life. She was at home in Pacifica when she called. Her voice was laced with apprehension. "So what's up?"

I got right to it. "Ains, I got a message today through Ancestry. com. Hilary and I took the DNA tests. So did your mom. Let me just read it to you." By the time I got to *I was adopted by the Pehrson family in May of 1967*, we both were sobbing. I struggled through the rest of it.

Ainsley was stunned, to say the least. "That has to be him!" she exclaimed.

I told her about the DNA matches, particularly the Parent-Child one with Virginia. We had a good laugh about that.

She said, "I did a DNA test with *National Geographic* awhile back. I'm 99 percent positive Jeff is my son, but I should probably do the Ancestry test just to be absolutely positive."

She reflected. "As you know, Al and I never had kids."

Albert Nies and Ainsley were married in 1977. He was a Vietnam War veteran, a creative engineer and inventor, and an eclectic blues guitar player. Al also battled PTSD and diabetes. He passed away in 2000 at the too-young age of 55.

Ainsley's sorrow was evident as she said, "Al saw too much in Vietnam and the horrible things man does to his fellow man. He just couldn't bring a child into that world. He also came from a large family with lots of siblings. Of course, he considered Brittany and Jimmy to be his kids.

"Back in 1967 I gave my son up for adoption immediately. I saw him maybe for a few moments. I never thought it was my place to look for him. But if he ever wanted to find me, I've always been open to that."

The tears began to flow again. "I just can't believe this is happening now. After all this time, my son—my only child—is reaching out. It's only been a year and a half since III died."

III (pronounced "three") and Ainsley became soul mates a few years after Al died. III was brilliant, theatrical, and unique. An early computer programmer, he set up some of the biggest banks with their data processing systems, majored in theatre at Cal Davis, and then became a management consultant specializing in team building for an A-list of tech and communications clients.

III eschewed email and never owned a cell phone. He wore pants that didn't require a belt and refused to allow his photograph to be taken. He was an early fixture in the Haight-Ashbury community in San Francisco and put over half a million miles on his VW Microbus that he registered, of course, as "Mr. III."

III was named after his grandfather and father. As the third, the only part of his name that was truly his was III. So, after 26 years of waging war with the California courts and agencies, he ultimately prevailed, and his name was legally changed to III.

"As you guys know all too well, the Universe works in mysterious ways. To think I have just lost my second husband, and the child I thought I'd lost 52 years ago now has resurfaced and wants to connect with me at the time I need it the most."

Ainsley admitted she was having a hard time processing all this.

I offered, "How about I send you Jeff's message and the DNA matches? Take your time and sleep on it. I won't respond to Jeff until we speak again."

Jeff and Ains would later teasingly accuse me of trying to slow down the reconnection from an abundance of caution. Maybe you just can't take the lawyer out of the man.

Meanwhile, Brittany had been seriously stalking "Jeff Pehrson" on the internet. She emailed me her findings.

Dad, Jeff has his own Wikipedia page. He's a rock star! And he lives in the Bay Area. There's lots of photos of him on Facebook. There's no question he's Ainsley's son. I'm just freaking out about this!!!!

I took a look at his page and instantly noted his full name is *Jeffery Vernon Pehrson*. Another Vernon in the family! And his musical resume is astounding: Co-founded Box Set in 1989…20 years of touring Europe and the U.S. performing with The Dave Matthews Band, Lenny Kravitz, Willie Nelson, Hot Tuna, Bare Naked Ladies, Goo Goo Dolls…Bay Area Band of the Year…played with the Jefferson Airplane 50th Anniversary Band…in 2010 he joined a band called FURTHUR formed by Grateful Dead bandsmen Bob Weir and Phil Lesh. And on and on…

I felt like Mission Control and thanked God I was retired. Hilary was eager for updates and Brittany was sending us everything she was finding on Jeff. The excitement level was off the charts and the three of us were texting non-stop.

This is a bombshell of the best kind.

OMG how will this unfold? Like a movie hopefully with a happy ending.

Does he have kids?

I don't think so; he has a fiancée.

He's super liberal. Likes wine! All good.

Oh, what a gift for Ainsley. I just pray he's a good soul.

I have a good feeling. Was waiting for this day.

And on it went into the evening.

On Wednesday, Ainsley called me around noon. Hilary had spoken to her late the night before and had given me the heads-up. "She'd like very much to connect with Jeff, if he's up for it," Hilary said.

I had sent Ainsley Jeff's Wikipedia page and she was astounded that, like her, he'd lived in the Bay Area all his life and they shared a love for the same music. "I was a year behind Bob Weir in high school. He was in a band called the Warlocks, and I was one of their early groupies. Turns out there was another band with the same name, so Bob's group changed theirs to the Grateful Dead. Back in the day we loved to go see the Dead, Big Brother and The Holding Company, and Jefferson Airplane."

We settled on a game plan. I would send a reply to Jeff through Ancestry and promised to let her know the moment I heard back from him. You could cut the anticipation and anxiety with a knife.

Hi, Jeff. Thank you for reaching out to me. As soon as I got your message, I forwarded it to my wife's family. It would certainly appear that my wife's older sister is your birth mother. I've spoken with her and she would like to connect with you, if that is something you would like to do. She lives in the Bay Area. Here is my email address. Shoot me an email as far as next steps and what you would like to do. We can also get on the phone if you like. I can tell you our family is pretty excited about this. Best regards, Vernon "Casey" Gauntt. I go by "Casey."

Jeff would later tell me he could tell I was a lawyer by my carefully chosen words. Well, as I said before…

Bam! Jeff responded within minutes.

I can't thank you enough for getting back to me. The last 24 hours has truly been a whirlwind, and I've been completely overwhelmed, in the best way. I would very much love to connect with Ainsley, yes. I understand she lives in Pacifica, which is about 40 minutes from me.

I actually reached out to her yesterday with the most carefully worded note I've ever composed and sent it to her on Facebook Messenger as well as to her Acorn Consulting email address. I'd be truly grateful to connect with all of you as well.

For 52 years I've wondered about my natural family, and it feels so good to hear from you!

Please let me know how Ainsley would like to proceed. I understand this may be delicate for her, so I'm more than happy to do this in any way she feels most comfortable. Thank you so much, Casey.

He certainly sounded like a good, thoughtful guy. I quickly replied to Jeff and let him know I was going to forward his email to Ainsley and have her check for his FB message.

He'd clearly been doing his own research and come up with her name, email address, and where she lived. I also sent Jeff her personal email address and this information, which I thought was very important. *She has no other children, by the way. My sense is at this point it's all good if you two communicate directly and make contact. I'll double check with Ainsley. I'm happy, of course, to facilitate in any way. We look forward to meeting you, too, Jeff.*

I sent Jeff's message to Ainsley and to Hilary and Brittany as well. I also mentioned to Ainsley that Jeff was comfortable communicating directly with her at this point.

With things squared away on my end of the soon-to-be reunion, Wyatt's Little League game became a priority—with my cell phone in tow. After the game, I went for an early dinner with Britt, Ryan, and the boys at a casual Italian restaurant. Ainsley and Jeff dominated the conversation. Hilary continued to text us from Cabo, eager for updates.

Brittany was beyond excited to discover she has a fifth cousin.

And "Aunt Hilary" and "Uncle Casey" were over the moon.

At 5:44 p.m. my phone pinged. Ainsley had texted: *Just replied to Jeff on Facebook…took 45 minutes to write two very short paragraphs. I included my phone number…Still shaking…*

Ainsley called me a little after eight o'clock. Her son had called her as soon as he got her FB message, and they had spent the last two hours getting to know each other. I could pin a lot of amazing adjectives on her recounting of their conversation, but the one that shone through so brightly was "happy." Ainsley was over the moon. They had so much in common: their personalities, the way they talked, likes and dislikes.

Jeff also talked about his adoptive mother, Janice, whom he adores. Janice was the one who encouraged Jeff to look for his birth mother. Ainsley laughingly added, "Jeff is going to call me MommA, because, well, I am his first mother."

Postscript

Six months later, Hilary and I made our annual pre-Christmas pilgrimage to the Bay Area to be with Virginia, Ainsley, youngest sister Leslie, and her husband, David. We gathered for lunch at Virginia's assisted living community in Foster City, eager to finally meet our "new" nephew and his lovely fiancée, Sara.

Jeff could not have been more warm, loving, and compassionate. He was also gregarious, funny, and quite comfortable taking the lead in conversation as he shared some hilarious stories of 30 years as a band's front man. As he admitted, "Large audiences, all that time on the road...you see and learn a lot...there's not much room for shy or reserved."

Jeff was shocked when I told him James Taylor's middle name is also Vernon. "I'll have to mention that to him when I see him," he said.

He even knows my idol, James Taylor! The perfect nephew.

Ainsley passed around a photo of the sisters' grandfather, C.D. Tedrow, a prominent banker from Princeton, Illinois. We were stunned by the resemblance between Jeff and his great-grandfather.

I was seated next to Virginia, now 93. Her body is frail, and she has good days and not so good with her memory and ability to speak. This was a very good day. She couldn't take her eyes off Jeff throughout the lunch, and several times she grabbed my hand and proudly said, "That's my grandson!"

It didn't need to be said, she had lost her one grandson only to be reconnected with another ten years later.

What really moved Hilary and me were the affectionate looks, touches, and exchanges between Ainsley and Jeff. Pure love.

Jeff is family. He assumed his seat as though he had always been there. And we couldn't be happier and more grateful.

Ain't Ancestry.com grand?

THE LIGHT WE CANNOT SEE

I WOKE UP early and my first thought was of *All the Light We Cannot See*. As I'm sure many of you know, that is the title of a wildly successful novel written by Anthony Doerr in 2014 for which he won the Pulitzer Prize. It's the heart-wrenching tale of a blind French girl living in Paris with her widowed father, and of a young, orphaned boy growing up in Germany as Hitler comes to power. Their lives are irrevocably ravaged by World War II and their paths intersect. If you have not yet read it, I highly recommend it. But that story isn't what woke me up.

The book's title re-triggered some thoughts that had been rattling around in my head. We are mortal human beings occupying these vessels we call our bodies. Our brains and our senses are amazing tools and machines that can do so many things, but they are finite and can only do so much. We can only see and comprehend as much as our brains, aided by the machines we build, allow us.

The most brilliant mathematicians and physicists have developed theories and proofs that were inconceivable 100 years ago. Yet even their discoveries are limited by the capacities and limits of their marvelous minds.

Imagine for a moment all the things we cannot see. Beings,

worlds, parallel universes, and wormholes all around us—right in front of us—yet invisible to us because of our limitations. Some of the early Spanish explorers of the Caribbean islands wrote in their journals that the indigenous peoples didn't "see" their ships anchored off the coast because they were not able to comprehend such things could exist.

Theoretical mathematicians have proven there are at least 11 dimensions and suspect many more. What's going on in those other dimensions? Are there intelligent beings or energies occupying those realms?

My son-in-law, Ryan, sent me an article from the *New York Times* a few years ago that dealt with a "spooky" theory of quantum mechanics. I don't profess to remotely understand the theory, but here are a couple of ideas that jumped out at me.

Scientists in the Netherlands have conducted experiments in quantum entanglement that prove objects, even those separated by huge distances, can affect each other's behavior instantaneously. Particles previously entangled can be affected when one is acted upon, even if the width of the universe separates them.

I find great comfort in this. We as parents could not be more entangled with our children. We share so much in common, not only DNA but memories, feelings, emotions, and instincts. And most important, love. When we lose a child there is a very real and painful knowing and feeling of separation, of loss. We can't see, hold, hug, and cuddle them. Or at least, that's what we are taught to believe.

But what if, even though we are physically separated from the deeply entangled "particles," the pure essence of our children, and even though they are now somewhere else, either close or unimaginably far away, in another dimension, parallel universe, heaven, or even right here; what if we are still able to instantaneously interact with them and affect one another's lives?

Many of our spiritual healers have told us, "Jimmy is only a thought away." I take that to mean if we think about Jimmy, if we talk to him, or write to him, he can hear us. Shouldn't that work both ways? Shouldn't we be able to hear Jimmy if he is thinking about us?

The answer is, "Yes, we can." And I will even go a couple of steps further and submit that our loved ones are much closer to us and interact with us, and us them, in ways well beyond just thoughts.

Up next: I put this idea to a couple of Catholic priests.

PRIESTS, MEDIUMS, AND QUANTUM THEORY

What can be powerful enough to change your path—
To change your future?
An act of nature—an act of love.
Once this deviation happens
You find yourself on a new path—
Uncharted, unknown and stretching out ahead of you.

—Touch, Introduction to the "Reunions"
episode, aired March 22, 2013

THE DEATH OF a child is most certainly powerful enough to change our paths. In fact, I'm hard pressed to think of anything more powerful.

In the "Into the Light" chapter of *Suffering*, I describe our first reading with Tarra, the medium from Sedona, who was so very helpful to us. December 22, 2008, was a beautiful Sunday morning as Hilary, Brittany, and I drove over the bridge to Coronado, a quaint town across the bay from downtown San Diego. It had not escaped me that on this day, 38 years earlier, my father died.

As we were introduced to Tarra, we were struck by how normal she was. Nicely dressed, short in stature, wide of body, with no piercings, tattoos, purple hair or scarves, this middle-aged mother of two grown sons spoke with a thick New York accent. Her laugh was contagious, and though we were insanely nervous, we instantly liked her. We had not told her anything but our first names, not why we had come, what we were seeking. Nothing.

After a brief meet and greet, Tarra focused in on Hilary. She reached for Hilary's hands and quickly discerned, "You recently lost a son, James or Jimmy, and his death had been violent and unexpected."

"Yes," my wife whispered.

Tarra's concern was apparent as she told Hilary, "When Jimmy died a part of you split. A piece of your soul went with him." Tarra looked at Brittany and me. "This may have happened to you, too, but it's strong with Mom." She looked back at Hilary. "Jimmy's telling me he can't come into your dreams or make his presence known to you because he's afraid you'll embrace him and not come back. He sometimes sits on the bed, but he won't wake you. You aren't ready. You want to be with him so deeply, and he you, but you can't go, not now."

Brittany and I exchanged a quick, painful glance.

I thought of my dad. *A part of you split and went with him.* I will come back to this.

A few years ago, our good friend Marilyn Willison sent Donna Nakazawa's article, "Four Minutes with My Father," that appeared in the July/August 2010 edition of *More* magazine. Unfortunately, *More* is no more. (Sorry, I couldn't resist.) Ms. Nakazawa described her near-death experience (NDE) when the medicine she was given to treat a rare neurological autoimmune disease caused a sudden and very dangerous drop in her blood pressure. In her NDE she was reunited with her father, who had died 29 years earlier, when Ms. Nakazawa was 13 years old, in the same hospital. Call it coincidence, but he died on this very same date at the age of 42, the age she would, hopefully, reach in three days. Her father repeatedly told her in her NDE to "choose life!"

Reading Ms. Nakazawa's article brought to the surface something I'd been thinking about. People who undergo a near-death experience travel somewhere and usually witness something beautiful, full of light, deep love, and peace, and sometimes communicate with loved ones who have passed over. When they come back to life they are uniformly and forever changed, with a new awareness and elevated consciousness.

So, the process should work both ways, right? I mean, if someone close to death can go over—let's just call it "there"—for a few moments or even longer, shouldn't those who are over there be able to come back here for a few moments now and then?

I'm not talking about ghosts, the paranormal, or poltergeists. Well, maybe I am, but certainly not the spooky movie stuff. But if there is a portal, a wormhole, to connect us with those who have passed that is accessible to the near dead, then it only makes sense that the departed can access a similar pathway back to here.

In her book *Messages*—good read, by the way—Bonnie McEneaney wrote of so many loved ones, including her husband, who perished on 9/11 in the World Trade Center towers and came through to visit their spouses, parents, and kids to let them know they were all right and love was eternal. They sat on the beds, stood next to the bedroom doors, dropped pennies and quarters. I believe it all; it's happened to a lot of us.

Visits and messages from our loved ones are revealed in myriad ways. Jimmy was a playwright, and his favorite way to connect is to manifest elaborate synchronicities involving multiple characters and scenes. "Healing All Around" is a good example of how Jimmy rolls. So are our connections with Rabbi Regina Sandler-Phillips, detailed in the "Condolences" chapter and "Sent by a Rabbi" in the Bonus Stories. In *Suffering* we included several other iterations of Jimmy's mastery of the art of synchronicity in the chapters "Want to Go for a Ride," "The Ghostwriter," "Sax Man," "The Rabbit Hole," and "The Fraternity." Let me summarize two of those.

The Fraternity came about when seemingly random forces brought three of us dads who had suffered the death of a child together in San Diego. The day after Jimmy was killed, Richard Page, an attorney colleague of mine but not a close friend, called me. He said, "I'm so sorry about Jimmy. You are now a member of the worst fraternity there is, my friend, the fraternity nobody should ever have to join. You have no idea how hard it's going to be. But I do, and that's why I'll call you every so often to see how you are doing."

And he did. Richard's 18-year-old son, Alex, had been killed in a car accident seven years earlier, in 2001. He knew.

Richard called in December of 2010 to tell me he'd had coffee with Greg Post, whose daughter had been killed four months earlier in a horrific car accident, exactly two years after Jimmy was killed.

I made a mental note to reach out to Greg, but I didn't. Richard didn't know Greg, either, but he cold-called him anyway.

Three years later, Hilary and I were at Torrey Pines High School for Awards Night to hand out Jimmy Gauntt Memorial scholarships, which we had done for five years. We were first on the program. Next up was Greg Post to present the Amanda Post Memorial Scholarship.

Greg was right there, and we were both honoring and remembering our precious kids who had died on the same day, two years apart. What did I do? I took the coward's way out, sneaking out of the gym after my presentation.

Then three things happened.

Back at home, a spectacular sunset flooded the dining room where Rod Knutson's painting of our family covers an entire wall. Jimmy, dressed as a waiter, stands outside a restaurant under an umbrella, glowing in the sun's last rays, while the rest of us remained in shadow.

The next day I got an email from Bill Harris, a friend I hadn't heard from in years, saying, *My wife and I were at the Torrey Pines awards ceremony last night.* He praised my speech and how we've kept Jimmy's spirit alive. And then he hit me with this: *After Jimmy's memorial service I needed to do something beautiful in honor of Jimmy. Beside our house I created a landscaped garden. I look at our Jimmy garden every day and think of him and your family.*

The following day, we got a beautiful email from Maya, one of the recipients of a Jimmy Scholarship. She thanked us and wrote how much it meant to her. She also said that Marinee Payne, the Torrey Pines High School theatre teacher for years, has a tattoo on her forearm: *Doubt Is A Bad Idea.* It's a line from Jimmy's poem "Suffering Is the Only Honest Work." Maya wrote, *Jimmy's words have become a mantra for me and many other Torrey Pines theatre students.*

I immediately tracked down Greg Post's email address and reached out to him. Hilary and I had a two-hour coffee with Greg and his wife, Missy, and became fast friends.

Two months later, the Fraternity was born when Richard, Greg, and I met and discovered each of us has a tattoo memorializing our kids in their handwriting. Etched forever across my back is the title of Jimmy's "Suffering" poem and his signature: Jimmy.

Let's go next into "The Rabbit Hole." At that first reading with Tarra, Jimmy explained in detail his accident and how remorseful he was for drinking too much that night and trying to walk home in the wee hours. He also said, "You need to reach out to the driver of the car that hit me. He's having a hard time and trouble sleeping."

I have to admit that was the last thing on my to-do list. We knew it was an accident, but I just couldn't picture having a conversation with the driver, or that he'd even want to hear from us. So, I put that out of my mind.

Jimmy is nothing if not persistent.

Four months later, we got an email from our good friend Kim Higgins. She said her husband, Steve, had been playing golf the day before with some buddies. At the tenth tee, one of Steve's playing partners pointed to a young man working there and said, "Last summer Peter was driving to work just before dawn and struck and killed another young man walking on the road. He's struggling and having a hard time sleeping."

Stunned, Steve exclaimed, "Oh, my God! It was Jimmy Gauntt! I knew Jimmy his whole life. His folks are good friends of ours."

Three days later, Hilary had reserved tickets for us to see David Lindsay-Abaire's Pulitzer Prize-winning play, *Rabbit Hole*, at our local theatre. This was the last performance.

The play is about a young couple, Howie and Becca, whose four-year-old son chased their dog into the street. He was accidentally struck and killed by a car driven by a 17-year-old, Jason. Eight months later, the parents still struggled in different, incompatible, ways with their enormous grief.

The second half focuses on the driver, filled with pain and consumed by guilt and grief. He wants to connect with the parents and apologize. Howie refuses but Becca meets Jason, who is hurting as badly as they are. She says, "It was an accident, nobody's fault. Don't let this destroy you. You have your whole life ahead of you."

As we exited the theatre, wiping away tears, and headed for the car, I heard Hilary shout, "Ow! I think I was stung by a bee."

As I carefully pulled out the stinger, Hilary exclaimed, "I've never been stung before. I think somebody is trying to tell us something."

This was the last performance of the play at our local theatre. A boy is killed by a car eight months earlier, the exact length of time since Jimmy's accident. Steve seeing Peter at the golf course a few days earlier. *He's struggling.* Coincidence?

Hilary thought not. "We have to contact that boy!"

That night I crafted a letter to Peter, telling him we weren't angry at him, that we were so sorry that he and Jimmy had to meet on that road at that particular place and time, and that Jimmy is fine, happy, in heaven. That Jimmy wanted him to be okay, as we each have a full life to live. That he was in our thoughts and prayers and we wanted him to be well. A month later we received a beautiful letter from Peter full of gratitude, deep emotion, and unburdening.

I also contacted David Lindsay-Abaire and told him how instrumental his play had been in convincing us to connect with Peter. Lindsay-Abaire replied: "It is my deep belief that through connection we heal. Your story is testament to that idea. I've been extra lucky to receive some nice reviews, and some significant prizes…. But I have never received something so humbling, and so gratifying, as the letter you've sent me."

I'm choosing to call these messages, sightings, and synchronicities near-life experiences—or NLEs. Jimmy's visits were not random. They were meticulously and divinely planned, and there were multiple purposes behind each of them; some of them obvious, while others took some time to be revealed.

Ask any of the players involved and they will uniformly tell you of the otherworldly feelings they have experienced from having touched or been touched by NLEs: hair standing on end, bodies full of goose bumps, dissolving into tears of wonder and joy. They say these experiences have changed their lives, their thoughts and views of what's next, over there and here. Very similar to the reactions of those who have had a near-death experience.

As far as I know, I never had an NLE before Jimmy died. There was nothing after my father's suicide. So how come these NLEs came flooding in after Jimmy left us? Why now? What makes them happen? What forces are at play? I sought out the help of two Catholic priests for answers to these questions.

Though I'm not particularly religious, I shared several of the stories of our NLEs with Father Patrick O'Malley in Chicago, whom I met in 1967. I was introduced to Father Pat by his two older brothers, Tom and John, both of whom worked for my grandfather's construction company, Case Foundation.

I had recently put the Vern Case story up on our website, Write Me Something Beautiful, and sent it to John O'Malley, who had risen to become the long-term president of Case. John sent the story to Pat, and that's how we reconnected in 2011.

I first sent Father Pat "The Letter." In his reply he wrote, "The story is captivating. Swiss psychiatrist Carl Jung said there are no coincidences. He called what you experienced synchronistic, which I always took to mean that some force, some power is at work in our lives in a way we can hardly imagine."

As a priest, he had another name for that force: God. He referenced the connection among all things, now proven by quantum physics. He also observed, "I recall the words of Jesus: 'The Kingdom is here!' I think you experienced it in a very profound way." *Heaven here on earth.*

It's interesting that Father Pat would invoke quantum physics, synchronicity, and the interconnection-entanglement of all things that we touched upon in "The Light We Cannot See."

I also sent Father Pat the stories "The Fraternity" and "The Rabbit Hole."

In retirement, Father Pat worked with seminary students in need of spiritual direction. One young man asked, "How do you know when you are making any headway in the spiritual life?"

Though he hadn't explicitly considered that question before, Father Pat came up with an answer that surprised him. "When you are a beginner in the spiritual quest, things happen. And it is only on later reflection that you say, 'That really was a God moment.' As you go along you begin to recognize the God moments ever more readily. Pretty soon, you are almost anticipating them—and they occur in greater numbers than you ever realized.

"Casey, is that what is happening to you and your friends in your Fraternity? Has the tragedy of lost loved ones moved you to a different plane, with different understandings? Is Jimmy at work in your life? Something is happening in your lives that you need to continue to look at."

In May of 2009, we attended a good friend's funeral. Bill Driscoll and I were fraternity brothers, both ways. We were Delts at the University of Southern California, and he and our dear friend Ludie, Hilary's sorority sister, lost their 17-year-old son, Brian, to heart disease in 2001. Monsignor Clement J. Connolly presided over Bill's service, as he did over Brian's, at the Holy Family Church in Pasadena. His sermon exuded warmth, humor, and a wisdom I found refreshing and captivating.

I sent the monsignor "The Letter" and "The Rabbit Hole." His reply personified his deep empathy and thoughtfulness: "There is a world beyond our knowing—in rare and sacred moments it is revealed to us. There, God dwells. From that place of mystery Jimmy is ever present to us. It takes pensive moments, a convergence of unexpected miracles and then the eyes of faith to see and feel and experience the Gospel according to Jimmy. Thank you for your blessing of sharing."

When the San Diego County medical examiner showed up on our doorstep with the news of Jimmy's death, I experienced a profound, literal, physical and painful reality that a piece of me was ripped out. Losing Jimmy broadsided me, knocked me off the track I'd been traveling down the past 58 years. I was now on an entirely new path, *uncharted, unknown, stretching out ahead of me.* Another life, one without Jimmy being physically present with us, had begun.

I completely understood that part of me died, split, and went with Jimmy. The piece of my heart that went with him left a vast hole. I'm pretty sure the same thing happens to all of us who have suffered the death of anyone we love deeply and dearly.

I'm calling these partial-death experiences, or PDEs. Unlike a near-death experience, the part of us that dies and goes with our loved one does not come back. Initially, all I could see was darkness and all I could feel was excruciating pain. From now on, life would be hell. There would never again be any true happiness, peace, or normalcy. We would never overcome our suffering and grief; the weight on our chests would ultimately suffocate us. We might even welcome our own death to be reunited with Jimmy.

Our child has died. What is life's relevance, its purpose? What is the point? Why slog along in this dimension, this so-called reality, pretending that nothing has changed and life simply goes on? We have visited life's darkest caves. Experienced in real, surreal, time the worst thing, the most imaginable nightmare that could ever come into our dreams.

We don't fear our own deaths. Our children have prematurely and unnaturally suffered this fate. It would be blasphemous for us to speak of dying with such trepidation.

What I could not possibly fathom at the time was that the part of me that died and went with Jimmy somehow, some way, created a bridge—a portal—that keeps us connected. And the hole in my heart would become an integral part of the instrument—in Jimmy's case a pen—that he can play and write through. It was also impossible for me to comprehend or envision that his death and my partial death could become a conduit for beauty, wonder, and even joy.

And if we apply quantum theory to our loss, even though we are physically separated from our loved ones, from their soul and all the pieces of them that crossed over, either somewhere near or unimaginably far away, we are still able to instantaneously interact with them and affect one other.

I've reflected more deeply upon Father Pat's and Monsignor Connolly's astute observations.

- The tragedy of lost loved ones has moved us to a different plane, with different understandings.
- My Fraternity brothers-in-loss now travel upon a different path that others can't understand.

- Our loved ones are at work.
- There is a world beyond our knowing. In rare and sacred moments it is revealed to us.
- Our loved ones are with God.
- They reveal themselves and their everlasting love and connection with us through pensive moments and convergences of unexpected miracles.
- We must have faith and open our hearts to what our loved ones want to show and share with us.
- There is heaven here on earth.

Mark Nepo's *The Book of Awakening* holds one of the most poignant quotes I've run across: "Once we pour ourselves into loving another person, it seems as if they take who we are with them when they go. In truth, they take a deep part of us…In every space opened when what we want gets away, a deeper place is cleared in which the mysteries can sing. If we can only survive that pain of being emptied, we might yet know the joy of being sung through."

This chapter is dedicated in loving memory of Father Patrick J. O'Malley, born to eternal life on July 5, 2013.

[In the Appendix we include some tools for receiving more God moments.]

HEAL: "WHAT DOES THAT EVEN MEAN?"

A FEW YEARS ago, I was having dinner with a friend and business colleague of mine, Edward. We were talking about our mutual loss and grief, and I mentioned the "H" word. Edward paused and with an uncharacteristic edge said, "Heal. What does that even mean?" He wasn't expecting an answer, and I didn't have one ready.

That's not the first time a bereaved parent has bristled, or gone on the defensive, when the words "healing" or "heal" entered our conversation.

I met Edward in 2016. He was working as a consultant for the company I was with at the time. After three days of meetings, he came into my office to say goodbye. He noticed the acoustic guitar hanging on the wall behind my desk. I showed him the autograph: "4 Casey, James Taylor," and explained that my nephew was at a concert of his in Lucerne, Switzerland. He'd brought the guitar I had given him the year before on the off chance there would be an opportunity to ask Mr. Taylor to sign it for me. Chutzpah.

"Wow." Edward was impressed. Me too.

He then turned around and looked at the photos hanging on

another wall. One showed James Taylor and two others showed our son Jimmy, our sweet baby James, perched on old beat-up trucks. I don't know what it was specifically. Maybe the way he was studying the photos. The day before he had mentioned, in passing, that he had a 13-year-old son. I didn't talk about my kids. But now, my antennae were up.

I pulled from my bookshelf a copy of *Suffering Is the Only Honest Work* and handed it to Edward.

"I want you to have this. My co-author, Jimmy, the one in those photographs, is my son. He was accidentally killed eight years ago. He was 24."

Edward held the book in both hands and stared at the cover for quite some time. His shoulders began to shake. He finally looked up at me and, with tears streaming down his face, said, "My son had a twin sister, Rhianna. She died three years ago. She was only ten. I'm barely able to talk about it and I sure as hell can't even begin to write about it."

Writing is what he does for a living.

We dispensed with the customary goodbye handshake and hugged. The next day he let me know he'd read the book on the plane ride home, but with a caveat: "I'm not ready to talk about it."

We were in different places. I was eight years into life without my child, and he was only three years into his.

Heal. It sounds simple, but the word is complex, and the 10th Edition of *Webster's Collegiate Dictionary* accords it four definitions. The most common: "To make sound or whole."

If to be *healed* means becoming whole again and restored to the person I was before Jimmy died, then, no, I am not healed. Nor will I ever be. I can never be *made whole.* Sure, there's a lot of me that's the same, but I've changed. The piece of me that split and went with our son is not coming back. The stuff that has poured in to partially fill the hole in my heart is new and much of it unrecognizable to my friends and colleagues. I'm not that person they remember and would like to have back. I can't go back.

That is only one definition of "heal," yet it is the one so many want for us. They want us the way we were before "it" happened. But, bless their well-meaning hearts, that just isn't possible. A doctor can't make it all better. There will be no "aha" moment when we wake up one morning and can say, "Okay, I'm finally healed. Whew. Glad that's over. Don't have to think about that anymore."

And we sometimes bristle when we hear the word, with that definition in mind, because we know at our core this is a finish line that can never be crossed. We become defensive when a colleague wants to know how we're coming with getting back up on the horse.

We're constantly confronted with the possibility that we're just like Sisyphus pushing that rock up the hill to reach the "all healed" summit, only to have it roll back down on us. Over and over again.

We think, "Something must be wrong with us. They feel sorry for us, even a little disappointed. We have let them down."

There's nothing "wrong" with us. We are simply different.

Webster's has another definition: "To cause an undesirable condition to be overcome: MEND."

Mend: I like this a little better. It speaks to survival, becoming able to live with and after the death of someone we deeply love, but never forgetting or completely adjusting to the loss. Healed to a point.

I'm reminded of the Richard Harrow character, a professional assassin in the *Boardwalk Empire* TV series. Harrow, played by Jack Huston, lost half of his face at Verdun during World War I. He wears a mask to hide his hideous wounds and make it easier for people to look at him. But his mask can't hide all his scars. He can only speak with one half of his mouth, all that's left. His wounds mended, to a point. His mind and psyche, not so much. He cannot forget his "troubles." Nor can anyone who looks at him and his mask.

I wear a mask. With it on I can smile, laugh, engage in light, breezy conversation with the best of 'em. I don't often let our friends and colleagues—and even some family—see the pain, my scars, my tats, my tears, the hole in my heart. I suppose, like Harrow, I want to make it easier for them. Easier on their eyes, their minds. But they know. They "see" the mask and out of respect, love, guilt, fear, or ignorance don't look away. They don't—can't—ask me to take it off. There are those few rare exceptions when someone will ask, "How are you really doing, Casey?"

And I'm okay with that.

Because I'm now okay with taking off my mask when I decide the moment is appropriate. I'm not afraid or uncomfortable to show and talk about my battle scars. This is how I can connect deeply with those I care about and love here and over "there." And deeply connect with people I have just met.

By taking off my mask with someone, and sharing my truth, my bad thing, I invite them to share their truth, whatever is weighing heavily on them.

On my plane ride back from my 50th high school reunion in suburban Chicago—Class of '68 is Great!—I chatted with my seatmate, a doctor at University of California San Diego. I mentioned that our daughter, Brittany, works with the suicide prevention team at UCSD. Dr. Kathy was familiar with it. She then popped the question, "So, do you have other kids?" I told her about Jimmy.

When I opened that door, Dr. Kathy leapt through. She told me she had lost two husbands and was battling her own serious health issues. Her suffering was palpable.

I gave her a brief version of our story, "The Letter," and how that led to a website and a book. I had a copy of *Suffering* with me and I gave it to her.

Dr. Kathy exclaimed, "You just have to meet Susan Hannifin-MacNab. She lives in San Diego. She lost her husband in 2012. She was 41 and their son, five, and she wrote a fabulous book, *A to Z Healing Toolbox*. I'll connect the two of you."

She did, and Susan and I have become good friends. In addition to writing and counseling others in grief, she is Programs and

Education Manager for Soaring Spirits International, a global support organization for the widowed.

Although Susan was motivated to write her book by her experiences as a widow, it is truly helpful for anyone who has lost a loved one.

Tom Zuba wrote the foreword to Susan's book. He has walked the walk. He not only survived the death of two children and his wife, Tom's excruciating experience with grief and healing has evolved into a life's work of helping others all over the world who are living with the death of those they deeply love. His book *Permission to Mourn* is at the top of my highly recommend list, particularly for the guys.

In his foreword, Tom writes, "Is healing possible? Healing your broken heart? I believe it is. But I don't think healing is always a destination at which we arrive. For many of us, healing becomes our way of being in the world. The work of healing is hard...In order to heal you have to work at it. Many times throughout the day."

Healing isn't a destination...healing becomes our way of being in the world. Zuba's words resonate deeply with me. Healing isn't a chore you check off your to-do list. Healing is a way of moving forward in our new lives on our new uncharted paths. It becomes a necessary part of our daily life.

The work of healing is hard. We can surely attest to that. It's akin to going back to school and taking classes taught in a completely foreign language. Or starting a new job with absolutely zero experience. We learn as we go.

Tom went on to write, "Susan and I talked about hope. And possibility... We talked about the importance of holding a vision of what healing looked like. So, we would know it when we arrived. At a place of healing."

I readily admit, in those initial years after Jimmy died, it was impossible to visualize myself *arriving at a place of healing* or think something like that was even remotely possible.

A couple of years ago I was talking at our gym with Guillermo, an overly confident Cuban-born and exiled attorney friend of mine. The 26-year-old son of a close friend of his had recently died from an accidental drug overdose. Guillermo asked me, "When did you feel you turned a corner with your grief after Jimmy died?"

Thoughtful question. Quick, though truthful, answer: "It was when I felt I was in a place where I could begin to help others. I started the Fraternity with a couple of other dads and became more comfortable sitting down one-on-one with parents, listening, sharing our pain and experiences, and providing some guidance and support. That wasn't until five years after Jimmy died."

I can't say I knew then, or even know now, what healing looks like, but I knew I had arrived at some place, some milestone, with my healing.

For five years our loss consumed me. Sure, some amazing things were happening to us early on, like my father's letter, incredible synchronicities, and visits from Jimmy. And I was feverishly writing them down and sharing them with others, protecting myself behind emails and our website. But I was not yet at a place where I felt I could sit down face-to-face and companion others with their loss. My pain was too fresh, too self-absorbing.

George Blystone was my best friend in high school. After a 25-year hiatus, our friendship was rekindled in 2010, thanks to another one of Jimmy's masterpieces. That story is told in the "Want to Go for a Ride" chapter in *Suffering*. George and Ann's 34-year-old daughter, Remy, died four years later, in 2014. We recently addressed the question: How can you tell if you are healing—getting better? We both agreed healing may best be measured by looking back and comparing where we are now to where we were at ground zero. George waxed poetic, "On any given day, you may not think you are very far along, but over time you begin to appreciate the difference."

Dr. Alan Wolfelt, in his book *Companioning the Bereaved*, states the truth that "grief never resolves. While we can learn to reconcile ourselves to it, grief is transformative and life-changing…The grief journey requires us to spend time with depression, anxiety and loss of control. It requires going into the wilderness."

When a child or anyone we love deeply dies, we find ourselves thrust into completely new and foreign territory. It is a wilderness. Frightening, lonely, wild, foreboding to be sure. But also filled with amazing, beautiful, mind-bending things we couldn't really see before.

Dr. Wolfelt says it is within the solitude of the wilderness where our heart is invited "to observe signs of sacredness, to regain purpose, to rediscover love, to renew life!" It is in the wilderness where we can find and interact with "the mysterious, spiritual dimension of grief that allows us to go on living until we, too, die."

So, back to the question: Heal. What does it even mean?

I agree with Tom, Susan, and Dr. Wolfelt. Healing is possible, but we will never be healed. Not in the sense that we can ever become whole or the person we were before. We will never forget the loved ones we lost, and the pain will always be there, but hopefully less intense as the years go by.

The first stage is taking care of yourself and your immediate family: your spouse, your kids. That's all-consuming. We called it "doing the work." Hilary, Brittany, and I were Team Healing. We saw therapists, mediums, shamans, psychics, Indian guides, tarot card and coffee ground readers. We participated in psychic-led grief groups. We read all the books, listened to the tapes. We did it all! Still do.

Five years after Jimmy died I was in a place, a stage, where I could begin to help others. My writing evolved from sharing our experiences— storytelling—into more pragmatic, introspective pieces about grief and loss. I've ventured well beyond the remnants of my former comfort zone to take deeper looks into what might be going on with our visits and synchronicities, and help others prepare and open up to receive theirs. I've written and spoken very publicly about my father's suicide, something I never thought I'd be able to do.

Is there another healing place/stage for me? Who knows? I'm content to continue doing the work. Every day.

I do know our exploration in the wilderness of the *mysterious, spiritual dimension* of grief has helped me and my family get to a healing place I never imagined possible when we were at ground zero. As I know it has helped so many others.

In this place there is still sadness, tears, and tough days, but there's also happiness, joy, laughter, new adventures, new hobbies, and the incomparable blessing of new life in the form of our two grandsons and a granddaughter who will soon make her debut. And there is always love.

Healing is part of who we now are. For many, like Tom, Susan, and Dr. Wolfelt, healing and helping others has become a way of life. Our healing evolves with us, those close to us, and those we encounter when our paths cross. There are yard markers, but no goal lines. And, although the rock of grief will sometimes slip, if we work hard at our healing, every day, we can at least keep it from rolling back to the bottom like poor Sisyphus.

P.S. Edward is now at a place where he is talking and writing beautifully about his amazing daughter, Rhianna. This chapter is dedicated to her memory.

BEN

THIS STORY WAS shared with me by Melinda Bay, a childhood friend and a chaplain in a large Chicago hospital. She was working the evening shift when a young man, John, was brought into the emergency room around ten that night. His motorcycle had been broadsided by a car that ran a stop sign. He was in very bad shape. He had regained partial consciousness but was unable to answer questions.

Bay found his parents' number in John's phone and called them, briefly explaining the situation and asking pertinent questions. "Please come as soon as you can."

Thirty minutes later they arrived, shattered and frightened. Their son knew they were there but was unable to communicate except by squeezing their hands. After multiple tests, John was transferred to the intensive care unit. Minutes later he coded, medspeak for his heart stopped. Doctors were able to regain a heartbeat, and he was intubated and sedated.

As Bay sat with his folks, she found out he was 27 years old, an only child, single, and working on building his own architecture business. His parents said John had never completed medical or financial powers of attorney. Bay helped them fill out those forms, naming his mother as surrogate.

John's brain was bleeding, but he was not stable enough for surgery. His MRI showed two pre-existing brain tumors, which the neurosurgeons were quite sure were malignant. His parents agonized over decisions and had countless meetings with multiple doctors over the next 24 hours. Finally, they operated to stop the bleeding, and a drain was inserted to relieve pressure on his brain.

They also reduced John's sedation slightly, hoping for any chance of improving their ability to communicate with him. A few hours later, John was able to squeeze hands and then whisper. More bad news came as the cardiologist informed his folks that John also had a pre-existing heart condition that would require surgery as soon as he was strong enough.

At three p.m. the next day, Bay began her next shift. John's parents immediately updated her on his condition. John was stable, and Bay encouraged them to go home and get some rest, promising to check on their son and call them if there were any changes.

Bay checked on John several times that evening. They talked a bit when he was awake and he whispered to her that he had completed a Do Not Resuscitate form that evening. John said he just could not do that when his parents were there and he would talk to them about it tomorrow.

Before the end of her shift Bay checked in on John once again, but he had a visitor with him, a man wearing a red flannel shirt in spite of the July heat. Bay asked John if he needed anything, waved to them, and said good night. She saw his nurse and asked her if she had seen John's visitor. The nurse said, "I thought maybe his parents had called a friend of his. I didn't want to interrupt them."

When Bay returned to the hospital the next afternoon, she found a note on her desk summoning her to the ICU immediately. She found John's parents sitting in a waiting area outside his room. They said he'd been sleeping all day, so they had not been able to talk with him. That morning they had received a phone call from friends in Wisconsin. The previous day their son, Ben, was tragically killed in a logging accident in Michigan. John and Ben had been best friends since childhood and were planning to go into business together, with Ben supplying the lumber and John designing log homes.

John's parents were afraid to tell him about Ben's death, not knowing how he would respond. Bay's brain was spinning as his parents continued to talk about whether to tell John. When their phone rang, she took the opportunity to check on John. Bay then walked down the corridor to the ICU lobby and placed a call to John's nurse from the previous evening. Bay asked her if she had seen John's visitor again. The nurse said, "No, but during John's restless sleep, he mentioned 'my friend Ben' a few times."

John's current nurse appeared in the lobby and interrupted the call, urging Bay to come back to John's room. John was awake and his parents were in his room. His mom was on the floor and his dad had crumpled onto a chair. Neither could speak. Bay called for help, and while a nurse and the intensive care doctor checked them over, Bay tried to talk to John. Barely coherent, he said Ben had visited him the night before and he knew Ben had died earlier that day. When John told his parents of his friend's impossible visit, they both collapsed.

John squeezed Bay's hand, signaling he wanted to say more. She leaned in and he whispered, "Do you believe me?"

"Yes."

His body relaxed. He looked at his parents and then back at Bay as if to say, "Help them."

His mother was feverishly digging in her purse and pulled a picture out of her wallet of John and Ben, John in a suit and Ben in a red flannel shirt. She said, "It's a recent picture taken to use on their business cards and brochures."

Bay nodded as she looked up from the picture and into the mother's imploring eyes. John's visitor the night before was Ben.

Bay texted the photo to John's nurse from the night before, and she confirmed that Ben was the man in John's room.

Bay's shift was almost over and she briefed the night chaplain, who went to another room to care for John's parents. Bay sat with John. He said Ben's name a couple of times. Then he beckoned Bay to come closer so she could hear him say, "I have to go. Don't let my parents come in. They'll make it harder."

Bay asked, "Do you want me to stay?"

"No. I'm not alone."

Bay offered a brief prayer and left as he slipped into unconsciousness. She stepped out of the room and encouraged his folks to go in and talk to him about whatever was in their hearts. Though their son never responded, they knew he heard them. John passed peacefully that night, leaving love as well as grief for those still here.

[*Note: For privacy, actual names have not been used.*]

I KNOW YOU THINK THIS WILL NEVER GET BETTER

FOR MANY, MANY years I did my best to avoid talking about my father or his death. It was just too painful. Although very rare were the times I did talk about my dad, never was it more vitally important than that night in 1982. Here's the back story.

In the fall of 1973 during my second year of law school at the University of Southern California, as was the custom, I interviewed on campus for a summer clerkship with several Los Angeles law firms and was invited back for more extensive interviews to a few of them, including the mid-sized corporate firm of Hahn Fraser. The last of my full afternoon of interviews was with the senior name partner, Horace L. Hahn. Mr. Hahn was 55 years old—hard to believe I'm now 15 years older than him as I write this. I was a baby-faced 23-year-old married a whopping three months.

I was seated opposite him at his leather-topped desk occupied by a couple of neat stacks of papers and an ashtray full of butts of unfiltered Chesterfields. The walls of his corner office were paneled in dark oak and the windows covered with shutters made of the same wood. Mr. Hahn was ruggedly handsome, with close-cropped reddish-gray curly hair, broad shoulders, military-like posture, and a booming voice and boisterous laugh. Although I rarely pay attention to these kinds of things, I noticed the gold ring on his right hand—two eagles with their wings outstretched perched on opposites sides of a diamond. He spoke with an air of aristocracy. I instantly liked him.

We chatted for a few minutes about this and that, and then he became very serious. He leaned forward with both forearms on his desk and, with his wolf-like gray eyes boring into mine, asked—no, demanded to know—"Mr. Gauntt, what is the worst thing that has happened to you in your life?" I was momentarily stunned by the question.

No one in my other interviews asked me that. In fact, no one before had ever asked me that. There was no doubt about my answer, only a brief hesitation of whether to take the easy way out—"Uh, I didn't get into Stanford Law School"—or open the door to the dark basement I rarely entered.

Keeping my face expressionless, I replied, "My father died by suicide a few days before Christmas in 1970. He ended his life at his office the night I came home for the holidays. I was 20 years old and a junior at USC."

I can't specifically recall what either of us did next. But what I do know is at that moment a bond was formed between Mr. Hahn and me that would become stronger over the next 30 years, right up to his death. Horace Hahn, who had no children of his own, became like a second father to me. I wear his eagle ring every day. Oh, and I got the job.

Shortly after starting at Hahn Fraser as a full-time associate in September of 1975, I began to work with Brian, a senior associate specializing in everything that wasn't litigation. I worked closely with him, and he trained and mentored me in a wide variety of interesting real estate and corporate matters.

Brian, a very bright, hardworking, energetic, and excitable

lawyer, was impulsive and prone to fits of temper. He liked to get a drink or two after work and he asked, or actually dragged, me along many a time, much to Hilary's chagrin. There really was no such thing as one or two with Brian. More like five or more, always scotch and sodas.

This after-work time spent with Brian was invaluable. I learned everything about firm politics, how the partnership worked, the compensation system, what you had to do to make partner, how the personalities of the partners shook out, whom to work for and whom to watch out for. I also got all the gossip and details of what went on in the partners meetings.

Brian was also very ambitious. He made partner about a year after I started. His new client, Steve Bronco, about his age, also a lawyer, was starting a new bank. After a few drinks, Brian often railed against the injustice of his clients making so much money, far more than he was as a lawyer, when he was infinitely smarter than they. He swore they were piggybacking on his intellect to make their fortunes.

Brian also complained about being undercompensated and underappreciated by the firm, and he didn't care who knew it: his partners, me, anyone who'd listen. So in 1978 he left Hahn Fraser and set up his own firm. Steve and his new bank threw a lot of work to Brian, and in a short time Brian quit his law practice and went to work full time for the bank as general counsel, hoping to reap his fortune.

By the time Hilary and I moved to Solana Beach in 1979 and I went to work for Hahn Fraser's recently opened San Diego office, Brian and I had lost touch.

Three years later, the newspapers had a field day reporting that a criminal indictment for bank fraud had been filed by the U.S. Attorney in Federal Court in San Diego against Steve, Brian, and others.

One Wednesday afternoon in 1982, Brian called me from out of the blue and asked if I'd heard the news.

"Yes," I replied.

"I'm in San Diego. You have time to get a drink? I'd really like to talk to you, but it's short notice so if you can't, I understand."

"Sure. Where do you want to meet?" I asked.

His voice was subdued. "Well, actually I'm calling you from the bar in your building. I've been here a while."

A few minutes later I walked in. He was sitting at the bar, talking on the phone. We shook hands and he gave me the "one minute" sign. I found an empty booth in a corner and slid in.

When he got off the phone, he came over with his scotch on the rocks and boomed, "Casey Gauntt! How the hell have you been?" He snagged the waitress and ordered another. "What'll you have?" he asked.

"Dewar's and soda, tall," I said.

Brian asked about Hilary and our daughter, Brittany, who was two. He told me he and his wife, Maryann, and their two teenage daughters were still living in their fabulous house in Los Angeles, a classic, designed by Green and Green. We talked about Hahn Fraser and some of his former partners.

"I made partner two years ago," I said, wondering what his reaction would be.

Brian lit a Winston, and though I normally didn't smoke unless I went out for cocktails, I bummed one from him, the first of several that night. "Gauntt, don't you ever buy your own cigarettes?" he teased.

After a half hour of catching up, and a fresh round of drinks, the conversation turned serious as Brian laid out how the bank had tried to hide liquidity problems. "At first I didn't realize what was going on," he said. "Then I did. I should have quit right then, but I thought we could work the bank out of its financial problems before the regulators figured out what was really going on." He stubbed his cigarette out before admitting, "It was stupid, wishful thinking."

Which led to regulators seizing the bank. Brian was not only out of a job, but criminal charges had been filed against him and his cohorts. He swirled the ice in his drink as he said, "I'm broke, Casey. I've spent a small fortune, all my savings, on defense attorneys. I'm afraid I'm going to lose everything. We're gonna be homeless if something doesn't change."

He took a deep breath. "Okay, here it is. This afternoon my lawyers and I met with the U.S. attorneys handling the case and we cut a deal. I'll plead guilty to some felony charges and cooperate with their investigation against the others, and they'll recommend a sentence of five to eight. Could be more, could be less. Up to the judge. Bottom line? I'm going to jail." He slumped against the booth, looking beaten, defeated.

"When does this happen?" I asked.

"It'll take a couple of days for the plea agreement to be prepared and then several weeks before I go before the judge for sentencing. I'll lose my ticket, you know. When you plead to felonies the California Bar takes your license. I'll never be able to practice law again. Hell, I'll never get another job."

Brian stared into his near-empty drink for a long time and then looked sideways. He rubbed away tears that began to fall from his puffy eyes. His shoulders shook. "Casey, I screwed everything up. I've thrown it all away. Everything. My girls—how can I tell 'em? How do I go home and look at my family and say, 'Guess what? Daddy's going to jail.' Oh, for God's sake, how the hell can I go to jail? How do I do that?"

He got very quiet before he looked at me and said, "I can't."

His desperate look and the hollow sound in his voice told me he'd made a decision, one he'd probably been turning over in his mind for weeks.

The waitress approached with another round. I waved her off. Brian and I spent the next hour locked in the most serious conversation I'd ever had with somebody.

"Brian, I know this is bad. It's hard to imagine how you will ever be able to live with this or get beyond it. You think this will never get better; it will only get worse. But I need to tell you something and I'm speaking from experience. You know my father died by suicide, right?"

He nodded.

"I was 20. My sister was 13, in the eighth grade. Laura adored my dad. He was her favorite person in the whole world, her knight in shining armor, and she was his princess. Brian, you think if you check out that will make it better, easier, for your family. It won't. It'll be worse, for a long, long time. Maryann and your girls will be hurt and embarrassed if you go to jail, and they'll cringe when friends ask, 'Where's Brian?' 'Where's your dad?' 'What does he do?'

"Bad news spreads fast. Most of them already know. And your girls will deal with the questions, the disgrace. But, Brian, they may never be able to deal with the loss, the emptiness, if you check out. It's been 12 years since my dad took his life and I still haven't dealt with it. My sister hasn't. My brother hasn't. If you do this, you won't go to prison. But, believe me, you'll be handing your wife and daughters a life sentence."

I leaned closer. "I don't care how bad it gets for you. It will never come close to the pain and trauma you will bring onto your family if you do this. Brian, your family loves *you!* They want *you!* The rest of this crap will fade away. You have to ride this out for your girls."

Through our tears, we talked a little more and I encouraged—begged—Brian to check into the hotel next door. I walked him up to the check-in desk to make sure he did it and asked him to call me in the morning. I drove home, a stupid thing to do given the "couple" of drinks I'd had, but the adrenaline was pumping and all my senses were firing. I got to the house around midnight; my wife and baby were sound asleep. I climbed into bed hoping I'd get that call.

In the morning I awoke, exhausted and hung over, and was back at the office around eight. I debated whether to call or go over to the hotel and see if Brian was still there. I admit a big part of me was afraid to find out, so I ended up doing nothing, except worry.

A couple of hours later I got a call. It was Brian and he was back in L.A. He said he had gotten up early and driven home. He had just finished telling Maryann about the plea bargain, and they would tell the girls when they got home from school. He sounded pretty good. He said he'd probably be back in San Diego in a few weeks and maybe we'd get together then. He signed off with, "And thank you...for everything."

Brian ended up serving a little less than two years. I saw him a couple of times after he got out, the last at a retirement party for Horace Hahn in March of 1987. Shortly after his release, Brian went to work for one of Horace's longtime clients. He had stopped drinking and looked as fit as I'd ever seen him. Brian and Maryann were still together and his girls were doing well. He seemed happy. That was the last time I saw or spoke with Brian. He died of pancreatic cancer in 2002.

At around 12:30 p.m. on Friday, August 15, 2008, Hilary and I walked out of the Mandeville Auditorium on the UCSD Campus in La Jolla. The memorial service for Jimmy had just ended. We watched his friends, his pallbearers, lift his casket into the hearse parked next to the auditorium. Still shellshocked, we did our best to greet and hug as many as we could of the family and friends in attendance as far as the eye could see.

A woman, maybe in her mid-60s, approached me. She looked familiar, but I couldn't put a name to the face. I held out my hand to shake hers, but she gave me a hug instead.

"You may not remember me, Casey, but I'm Maryann. I'm here for you today because you were there for Brian and us all those years ago. Thank you, and God bless you and your family."

She walked away, wiping tears from her eyes, as I did from mine.

FOR NIKA

*To throw away an honest friend is, as it
were, to throw your life away.*

—Sophocles

HUGH SILL AND I reconnected in February of 2011 in a very
powerful way. A mutual friend of ours from New York, John Morehouse, facilitated the reunion. Hugh and I were fraternity brothers
at USC, picked pineapples one college summer in Maui with John,
a football player from Cornell, and we all became very good friends.
Hugh helped me a lot after my father's death. We did some business together in our 20s but by 1980, for reasons that are no longer
important, we fell completely out of touch.

At some point in the early 1990s I had learned that one of
Hugh's sons, as a toddler, had fallen into a swimming pool. George
was pulled to safety before he drowned, but the brain damage was
irreversible and he was severely and permanently handicapped. I
didn't reach out to Hugh then, nor when George passed away 10
years later.

John contacted me a couple of years after Jimmy died. He said Hugh had told him about Jimmy's accident shortly after it happened. John is no stranger to loss. His younger brother died of cancer in 1972, and then a sister and both parents. John knew of this loss Hugh and I had in common and our falling out. He felt compelled to do something about it. John told me later, "You guys were good friends, and I'm a firm believer in 'life's too short.' We can't let some negative things get in the way. Besides, I knew you could help each other."

It goes without saying, Hugh and I had a lot of catching up to do—and say to one another about our boys. And we did over phone calls, emails, dinners, and cocktails.

My correspondence with John and Hugh, in spite of our 30-year intermission, has been deep and very helpful and healing for me, and I believe for them, too. I've shared with them many of the stories on Write Me Something Beautiful, and they have in turn shared theirs with me.

A couple of years after our reconnection, Hugh sent me something that profoundly moved me to the core—the words he had spoken to the hundreds assembled in St. Francis of Assisi Church in Bakersfield for the marriage of his daughter, Nika. Words that can only be forged by one who has suffered heartbreaking tragedy and loss, and an evolved soul who can see beyond to the beauty and love that surrounds us all.

Hugh Sill wrote something beautiful.

FOR MY DAUGHTER NIKA ON HER WEDDING DAY

Thank you, Monsignor Craig, for this opportunity. I know for Nika and Jake it comes as a surprise my standing here, so I am sure they are a little nervous, but they need not worry as I have some experience at this. Six years before Nika was born, at a wedding in Australia, I spoke before a crowd similar to this today, and although

I did suffer a complete blackout during the speech, I was told by a few that it wasn't all that bad. So, I'm here to give it another try!

I want to thank all of you for being here today, in celebrating this marriage between Jake and Nika.

Just a few days ago the remarks that I had planned to give were completed. I had worked for months in trying to put together something that Nika and Jake would be proud of. I spent hours going over each sentence—every word—I wanted it to be perfect for this occasion.

I had planned to talk about the importance God has played in Jake's and Nika's lives. To tell you about Jake's family and the role they have all played in Jake's life. To mention my sons, how proud their mother, Carrie Ann, and I are of them for many reasons, but never more so than the time Nika brought home Jake to meet her brothers, and the two of them telling Nika, "He's the one."

To Karil, and how important he has been to our family and to Nika's growing up. How proud I am to see him standing as a groomsman for Jake next to my sons and daughter on this altar.

I wanted to tell you about the beautiful bond between Nika and her mother and just how fast Nika had to grow up watching two parents battle cancer and to witness every day a brother she loved so much, whose life was slowly slipping away in front of her eyes.

That was my goal—that was the plan—but in my heart I kept coming back to what brought me to this pulpit. It is a story I want to share with all of you, one that I might never have the opportunity to do again. Because this is who my daughter is, and this is the woman that Jake has fallen in love with.

Jake, you never met Nika's brother, George. He was an amazing young man who showed us all the meaning of courage. George didn't have an easy life, but it is George, and his life, that for me, makes this day so special.

You see, over and over again, I kept thinking about Nika when she was very young, six or seven. She would arrive home from school, walk through the door and always go over to George, lie next to him and proceed to tell him how her day had gone. George would have this big smile on his face; it was really all he was capable of doing in showing his appreciation. She would always want to help her mother and Karil, George's caregiver, in any way she could, but never did she forget to give George a hug and a kiss. Then as Nika grew older, she entered Garces Catholic School. Still, every day she would walk through the door and go right to George's bed, where he already had the big smile on his face, anticipating her arrival. She would lie next to him, tell him how her day had gone and, most importantly, always give George a hug and kiss.

Nika stands here today, now all grown up, and she once again touched my heart. Last Wednesday night we returned home from having dinner with Jake's dad. Upon entering the house Nika, as has been her ritual throughout this wedding process, went to the mail. She took special interest in a small package. She said it had become lost, was tracked down in Hawaii, and how happy she was that it made it in time for the wedding. I was intrigued, and when she opened a tiny box I couldn't tell what it was. She informed me it was a locket. I asked if this is another wedding tradition, like something borrowed, something new? She told me, "No, Dad, it is so I can put a picture of George in it to carry with me on my wedding day."

Nika was never uncomfortable with her brother, and always proud to introduce George to her friends who came to love him as she always had.

I mention this story not out of sorrow, as God gave us a beautiful and joyous son. In George's passing I always tried to find the importance in his life. God had to have a meaningful purpose. To me, and I hope to Nika and Jake too, they can see just how important George is to this moment here today. Jake, that beautiful young lady next to you who you fell in love with is the person she is today because of so many good people in her life, but also because of an unforeseen event that made Nika the person you now love so much.

George truly enriched our lives. In Nika, George brought out all the beautiful things in life that any father, mother, brother, sister, friend and yes, husband, would be proud of. I believe with all my heart that George is with us here today in Nika, through her love, her compassion, and her caring.

Jake, I know you have seen this, it is why we all love Nika so much, and I believe why you fell in love with her. As her father, I know I am somewhat biased, but I feel that if ever there was a person on this earth to be the best wife and mother, it is Nika.

Jake, as Monsignor Craig reminded me as I was preparing these remarks, this sacrament is about two people. I have stood here for several minutes and spoke almost entirely about my daughter, and I hope you will allow me a small amount of leeway as a proud father, but I know I can speak for Carrie Ann when I say that since the day you came into Nika's life we have never seen her so happy. Knowing you will be the one to protect her, to comfort her and love her on whatever path life takes you both, we could not be more honored in knowing it will be you by her side.

What a beautiful feeling to look upon all of you on this wonderful occasion and feel such happiness. To my beautiful daughter Nika, who today I am able to say that your entire family—yes, your entire family—is here, wishing you and Jake all the happiness life brings you.

Thank you, Monsignor.

Postscript

We published an earlier version of this story with lots of photos on our Write Me Something Beautiful website in 2013 shortly after Nika's wedding. As I was pulling this book together over the summer and early fall of 2020, I was thinking about what to include. "For Nika" was on my list as a possible chapter. Starting on September 22, I began to notice a big spike in the visits to the "For Nika" post on the website. It made me refocus my attention on that as a chapter. I reread the post and began to cry. I said to myself, "If Hugh and Nika are okay with it, this has to go in the book. Same for John Morehouse, since he's mentioned in the story."

"For Nika" touches upon so many of the messages we wanted to convey: the importance of healing and mending relationships and friendships no matter how much we believe they are broken; that it's never too late to express condolences to someone who has lost a child; and everyone has the capacity to love and help others while in their bodies, no matter the physical condition, and even beyond their lifetime here with us.

I emailed to Hugh and John a draft of the chapter on October 3, 2020, for their review and okay. Over the previous two weeks "For Nika" had received over 200 visits, and I mentioned this "coincidence" in my email.

John called me the next day. "Casey, I feel so bad, I thought you knew. Hughie passed on September twenty-first of pancreatic cancer. He was surrounded by his family."

John started crying and so did I. John had let me know of Hugh's diagnosis in August and I had reached out to Hugh on his 70th birthday a month before he transitioned. John and I spent the next hour sharing some of our favorite stories of Hugh and why we and everyone he ever met love him so much.

This chapter is dedicated to the loving memory of George Sill and his father, my friend and fraternity brother in college and in loss, Hugh Kevin Sill.

GIFTS FROM NICK

.

CONRAD LESLIE IS a good friend and a member of our Fraternity of Dads. He had a fairytale life: a beautiful home in Del Mar, California, a loving wife, and a son who was his best friend and the center of his universe. Conrad and his wife, Paola, were convinced they all would live happily ever after.

Their dream shattered on Bastille Day, 2016, the day an ISIS terrorist turned a 19-ton cargo truck into a weapon of mass destruction, careening into the crowds along the Promenade Anglaise in Nice, France. Twenty-year-old Nicolas, a junior at UC Berkeley, was studying abroad at the European Innovative Academy. As he and a group of university friends strolled and watched the fireworks, hell on wheels met him and 85 other celebrating folks, and Conrad and Paola lost their only child.

For three days after seeing the television news coverage, Conrad repeatedly called Nick's cell phone, hearing Nick's voice asking him to leave a message. Conrad convinced himself that Nick was safe, perhaps hiding somewhere until it was okay to come out. On the third day, he and Paola booked a flight to France. Maybe they could find him.

They tried to stay calm during a layover in Paris. They had

contacted the U.S. Embassy but got no helpful information. Since Nick held dual American and, thanks to his mom, Italian citizenship, Paola called the Italian Embassy. As they were waiting to deplane in Paris, Conrad's cell rang. An Italian official spoke the life-altering words that the Leslies can still hear: "We have bad news. Nicolas did not make it."

Paola and Conrad were both screaming as the other passengers got off the plane. The flight attendants tried to comfort them as they waited for their flight to Nice.

When they landed, the U.S. Consul in France, a representative from the State Department, a doctor, and some of Paola's family members from Italy were there to give them the terrible news in person.

The Leslies sank into a dark place, without hope of ever seeing the light again. Their hearts became black holes. "What ifs" plagued them. What if Nick had walked that way a minute sooner or had waited a minute to leave for the celebration? What if he hadn't been chosen to go abroad? What if, what if, what if? "What now?" was a question they were too wounded to ask, or even think about.

Yet life did go on, in a blur of grief and weeping. Paola, particularly, couldn't come to terms with Nick's senseless death. Then, upon their return from France, inexplicable "coincidences" began to show up.

But those are not my stories to tell. I'll let Conrad's words lead the way through the serendipitous events.

Our quiet beach community of Del Mar was a safe and beautiful place millions of miles away from terrorist attacks and other violence. A son of immigrants, my father a Cuban and my mother from Spain, I sought out this community because of the excellent public schools. For 23 years we paid a mortgage that seemed frightening, but it was worth sleepless nights and long hours at work since my son was receiving a great education. His elementary school, small with caring teachers and loving parent volunteers eager to help, had a 180-degree ocean view. Paola would bring hot meals to Nick for lunch. The school prided itself on being a global village, which helped Nicolas prepare for the world after graduation.

Nick graduated from Torrey Pines High School in 2014, a well-recognized and award-winning high school. He played lacrosse for the Torrey Pines Falcons, but in his senior year, he became interested in politics and joined the speech and debate team. He had natural skills in debate and soon rose to become the team's co-captain.

Nick was smart and athletic, confident without being arrogant. At six foot three and 190 he was tall and strong. At nine, he took up kitesurfing, and he became an instructor at 17. At ten he was certified as a SCUBA diver, moving on to free dive with sharks and night dive for lobsters. Black diamond ski runs held no terrors for him and his snowboard. Fluent in three languages—English, Spanish, and Italian—traveling abroad made him a true citizen of the world. He was always careful and prudent in everything he did.

Before the attack I loved life and feared death; I wanted to spend every moment with our son. I did not want the ride to end; I felt blessed. Was I pretentious or just naive to think that just because we had a good life and lived in paradise, destiny would allow us to live happily ever after?

After Bastille Day death became a friend to flirt with. Eventually my own death would be a ticket back to Nick. I lost my ambitions, my confidence, and my future. My career, my business, our home, professional recognition, suddenly became worthless. I no longer had an heir. The fruit of my love with my wife had been taken from us.

Life spiraled out of control. I started drinking. Paola faded into depression and complicated grief. "Why?" she asked over and over. My pain was already unbearable, and watching Paola suffer made it much worse, as if that could even be possible. We had nothing to live for, nothing to hold us together. It did not look good for us continuing as a couple.

As an engineer, I had never done much soul searching. My life plan was simple: go to college, study hard, get a good job, get married, have a family, and live happily ever after. I was never a spiritual person and had lost interest in my youthful pursuit of the meaning of life soon after I entered the work force. I certainly did not believe in miracles, mediums, or an afterlife. My reality was based on what I experienced physically, and the world made perfect sense to me.

Then things began to happen that challenged my worldview. We began paying attention to things outside the pain. Our magical ride toward the light began. Strange coincidences and perfectly timed synchronicities began to happen. Once I started to experience these things, I understood that there is something greater than this physical plane, something that lives and thrives after life. I have no idea what waits on the other side of the veil. I may never understand until it's my time to cross over. Yet since we've been paying attention to our "gifts from Nick," life has become amazing. These gifts are all about love and they arrive at critical times just when we need them the most.

One gift came while Nick was still with us, a year before he left for France. My mother, Conchita Zapata, came from Zaragoza, Spain. Without knowing a word of English, she brought me and my brother to the United States when we were very young.

In Spain, my mother was a celebrity, a champion of her native folk dance, La Jota de Aragon. Even the King of Spain honored her for promoting her home country in the Americas. Her portrait, honors, and some of her trophies lined the shelves in our reading room.

Paola and I sat on our couch watching a movie on television. Paola needed a quick break, so I paused the movie and waited while she walked past the reading room to the bathroom.

Suddenly she screamed!

"Are you okay?" I called.

She came in and sat down. "I had the weirdest experience," she said. "As I came back past the reading room, I felt a presence. I thought you were hiding to surprise me, you joker."

We laughed and I pressed Play. Suddenly, she grabbed my arm and looked up towards the ceiling. "I just heard a voice in my head. It said, 'Tell Nicolas that there is more life after life.'"

I gave her a disbelieving look. What she said was so odd and random in the middle of the funny movie we were watching. "You're weird," I said.

We looked at each other, laughed, and went back to the movie. A few minutes later the phone rang. A police officer was calling from the convalescent home in Los Angeles where my 92-year-old mother had been recuperating from her most recent hospital stay for several chronic conditions.

"I'm sorry to have to tell you your mother has just passed away," he said.

Shock doesn't begin to describe how I felt. We had recently visited her and she seemed to be doing well, although she had often said that she was ready to go, and that America was a strange country that kept people alive at all costs instead of letting them pass peacefully in their own time.

The policeman offered his condolences, then went on to tell me that I needed to make arrangements to have the body removed as soon as possible. "I can suggest some mortuaries if you want."

Still in shock, I hung up and went online to find a funeral home, gave my credit card number to the one I had chosen, and held on to Paola.

Several weeks after my mother's memorial service, we remembered the message Paola had received when we were watching television. It came through only a few minutes after my mother passed. We both agreed there could be no doubt the message was from Nicolas's grandmother. Should we tell Nick? Her death had been a shock to us all. He was in college and doing well. We did not want to freak him out. However, the message was intense and directed to him. We decided to tell him.

Nicolas did not believe in an afterlife. He believed that out-of-body experiences described during near-death situations were results of the drug DMT, a hallucinogenic secreted by the brain. He believed that this life was it, and since he was so good at debating, I could never convince him that perhaps there could be more.

Soon after we gave him YaYa's message—that's what Nick called his grandmother—*there is more life after life,* he began to meditate and take an interest in spirituality. Physics intrigued him, especially the quantum phenomenon of superposition, where one subatomic particle can exist at more than one place simultaneously. Quantum entanglement, two particles able to communicate instantaneously regardless of how far they were from each other, fascinated him. He studied Einstein's theory of the dilution of time, how time ticks differently between individuals based on the speed they are going or proximity to a strong gravitational force.

I believe the message helped prepare Nicolas for his last year on earth and certainly opened our minds to the possibility of afterlife communication.

Beverly is a friend of ours who is also a spiritual healer. One gray, overcast day, as summer fog blotted the light, we gathered in the living room so she could try to help Paola and me make sense of what had happened. Paola only stared and repeated, "Why? Why? Why?"

On the wall hung a 24" by 36" photograph I had taken of Nicolas that his friends had mounted on foam board for Nick's memorial. We had been kitesurfing in Del Mar and I came out of the water first. My picture captured Nick as he waded to shore, kiteboard in one hand, kite flying from the other, on what would be our last day kitesurfing together.

As Beverly spoke to Paola, my mind wandered, focused on the photograph. Random thoughts and memories rushed through my head. It was a beautiful photo, but the sun was behind Nicolas, the photograph was overexposed, and I could barely see Nick's features. Nick had such a big, beautiful smile and I wanted to see it again, a smile now forever lost.

The women's conversation became more intense.

Paola said, "Where's Nick?"

Beverly answered, "Nick is in the light."

Paola's voice rose. "What do you mean, Nick is in the light? Is he a light like a lamp, just hanging there in the sky for eternity? What kind of an existence is that? Where is he?" she demanded.

Beverly calmly repeated, "Nick is in the light."

Suddenly the sun broke thought the clouds. A bright beam shone through our skylights, illuminating Nicolas's face in a frame of intense light, whiting out everything but his face and his big, beautiful smile. I grabbed my phone and took a photograph just before the fog closed in again.

Words cannot describe what we felt. Nick truly was in the light.

Later I lay in bed thinking about Nicolas, crying quietly so as not to disturb Paola. I picked up my phone and scrolled to the photo I had taken. I whispered, "Nicolas, where are you?"

Siri's mechanical voice broke in on my sorrow. "I am right here," and the words popped onto the screen. I stared at the phone. Suddenly, a text message from Hunter, one of Nick's best friends, pinged. *I feel Nick is right here and that he left us so he could be closer to us and be able to help more of the people he loved.*

My question was answered. Nick is right here with me.

Before Nick had left for Nice, we talked about my plan to leave our house and business to him. Toward that end, a few years earlier we had bought a condominium in Kaneohe on the island of Oahu and rented it out until we needed it.

When I broke the great news, expecting excitement and thanks, he looked at me and said, "Dad, you don't have to worry about me anymore. You and Mom should sell the house and move to Hawaii! That's where you guys belong, and I want you to be happy."

Now the home we had loved for so many years had become a mausoleum dedicated to Nick's memory, where we would never be happy again. Why were we hanging on to it? To remind us of our pain? We didn't need reminders.

A couple of weeks later, my longtime tenant in Hawaii informed me that he was going to move out. This was the last thing that I wanted to hear. Dealing with a vacancy, hiring maintenance workers, finding a new tenant was too much. I just didn't care. The bank could foreclose and good luck to them.

Still, even though we had lots of good friends and an incredible support team, I could no longer manage the engineering company that I founded in 1999 or the mortgage, taxes, and other expenses related to our home. We were living off our savings.

Downsizing to our place in Hawaii made financial sense to me but more importantly, I believed the move would do us good.

We decided to rent out our home, and I hired a realtor to show it. However, after I signed the contract, Paola and I couldn't come to grips with letting the realtor and other strangers into our home. We just wanted to be left with our pain. After several months we gave up on the idea to move to Hawaii.

A few days after we made the decision to stay, our next-door neighbor came to visit. When I told her about our failed move, she eagerly blurted out, "I'll rent your house!" But she had one condition. We needed to be out by June first since they had already given their landlord notice. That was the same day our Hawaii tenant was moving out!

Coincidence? Maybe. Or as I believe, Nick was pulling some strings for us to make everything work out.

Though Paola agreed to move, she still struggled to let go of the home we both loved. Most of all, she was devastated and angry and still asking why this had to happen to us. Our arguments wore us out.

She felt that we had been singled out to suffer endlessly, that no one else had ever or would ever bear this burden of pain and loss. Nothing I could say changed her mind. Yet deep inside I felt that she was right. No one else could possibly own such anguish. The Universe had screwed us over but good. We had finished last in the tournament of life. In losing Nick, we lost our future.

Still, we plowed ahead. We hired a moving company for our personal items and some furniture. Most important to Paola was the couch where our small family had sat together in the evenings to watch a TV show or movie.

The movers arrived and began to work fast and efficiently. When they were ready for the couch, Paola stood by and supervised. She did not like the way they were packing it. "Put more padding around it," she insisted.

"Lady," one of the men said, "it's fine."

Although generally easygoing, Paola can be fierce when defending things that sparked memories of Nicolas and part of him was rooted in that couch. "Do it!"

The man shrugged and reached for more padding.

Her part done, Paola went to the bedroom and threw herself on the bed, weeping. Then a feeling came over her. She must apologize to the mover and explain why she had been so upset. She dried her tears and went to make amends.

She explained about Nick and how traumatic this move was.

The mover gave her a look of empathy. "Don't worry, ma'am. I'll personally make sure everything is safe."

At the end of the day, he came to me. "I owe you and your wife an apology," he said. "When your wife complained so much, it ticked me off. I thought she should have been in a good mood. After all, you're moving to Hawaii."

Tears filled his eyes. "I lost my only child several years ago and I know what you guys are going through."

I was blown away. Paola and I had been arguing about how we'd been singled out with our loss, and here was this mover, a stranger who came on our last day in our home, who was going through the same pain.

His simple words helped me accept the situation and surrender to the loss while finding gratitude. We were so fortunate to be able to change our lives by moving, a choice that perhaps this man who had worked so hard to pack our house did not have. In spite of his loss, which was equally, if not more difficult, than ours, he was still living his life.

Paola and I were both humbled by this synchronicity. The sorrow and pain from losing a child has been and will continue to be passed from family to family, as it has been since the beginning of human existence. I don't own this pain; I am only experiencing my piece of it. I am proud to belong to a loving Fraternity of helping fathers, which now includes our mover, who have lost a child.

We had always traveled as a family. My wife would rather build memories than buy expensive clothing, fancy cars, or luxury items. Paola was a pro at planning, and organizing trips brightened her days, so watching her in deep sorrow broke my heart. Maybe a trip to New Zealand, a place she had always wanted to visit, would lighten her grief. We booked the trip and landed on South Island.

One night as we slept, I had a vivid visitation from Nicolas. All three of us were together. Nicolas looked so solid and real. I instinctively felt we were in a room in an astral world and that I would eventually be pulled back into my physical reality. I fought against leaving and told Nick that I was going to stay and there was nothing that could separate us. I would remain in that blissful state with him forever.

Nicolas was the one who got up and started to leave the room. I frantically called out, "Do you have anything to tell me? What can I do here on earth to be reunited with you?"

Nicolas looked at me and smiled peacefully. His words materialized in my head. *Move forward, stay with Mom, and find joy.*

I awoke feeling as if someone had yanked me back through a portal. Happiness and gratitude flooded through me at being able to spend some time together in this magical place. I woke up Paola and told her every detail of what I had witnessed. "And Nick said, 'Move forward, stay with Mom, and find joy.'" What a wonderful message!

A couple of days later, we took a hike along the Blue River to the Blue Pools. The Blue Pools, named for their intense and unique color, are located at the junction with the Makarora River. When we arrived, the water looked inviting, but it was too cold to swim. The beauty of this special place engulfed us, and we decided to place a rose quartz crystal dedicated to Nicolas in the water.

As we stood on the water's edge, I wished we could share that magical place I had dreamed about with our son. Paola whimpered and started to break down. I held her hand and said, "Nick wants us to find joy. If we believe he is still with us, we need to listen to what he told me and find joy in life."

Seconds later, she looked at the ground. A small, round, flat rock glimmered in the light. She picked it up. On its surface a natural crystalline formation had made the letter "J" surrounded by a circle of white crystals. Joy. A rock of joy. Another message from Nick.

We were so buzzing with emotions that I plunged into the icy cold water. That's what Nicolas would have done. I think that he was telling us and the world that no matter how hard it is, every parent who has lost a child needs to somehow find joy again.

These stories are true. We've experienced many others. I can't prove that they were sent to us by our son, but I like to believe that they are gifts from Nick. These gifts have helped me learn about unconditional love, gratitude, and the joy of helping others, and put me on a path towards forgiveness.

I was taught at an early age to never give up, not to accept no for an answer, and to always focus on a solution rather than the problem. These traits helped me become successful in business. Now I have learned the importance of surrendering to something greater than me, something that I trust, yet don't understand.

I totally believe there is something more to reality that we can't see and don't understand. Wherever these signs come from, they have given Paola and me the strength to keep moving forward, stay together, and strive to find joy in life. I know that someone, somewhere, is doing some heavy lifting for us, lighting up a dark runway so that our spirits can take off. So that we can make it through.

My heart is still broken, and the depth of my sorrow is unimaginable, but my love for Nick continues to grow each day with every gift that he sends us. If we are indeed spiritual beings inside human bodies, with the objective of learning as much as possible from this physical world, I received the opportunity to experience the highest of highs being with Nick, and the darkest of depths living without him. I know without a doubt that I will see him again, we will be reunited, and that there is something larger than us, compassionate, intelligent, and full of love.

I will never be the same person that I was, but I like the new person that I am becoming. I have learned not to judge the whole by the small sliver of reality that I experience; at the end, the whole is perfect. Love never dies; and Nicolas and I are entangled for eternity.

Jimmy and Hilary, Grand Canyon 2005

Rogelio Ramirez with his grandson, Christian

Jimmy with his "big brother" John

Jimmy jamming with John Dale on guitar

Mary Sawyers Cook

Ainsley Nies and Jeff Pehrson

John and Ellen Morehouse with Hugh Sill, New York, 1975

Jimmy, Hilary, Brittany, and Casey, New Zealand 2005

Nicolas Leslie

Conrad and Paola Leslie

James Powell (L) with Jimmy Gauntt, Krakow 2005 (photo courtesy of PeterCunninghamPhotography.com)

Grover Gauntt Jr. and Jim Walton, Keeneyville, Illinois 1960

Casey with George Blystone

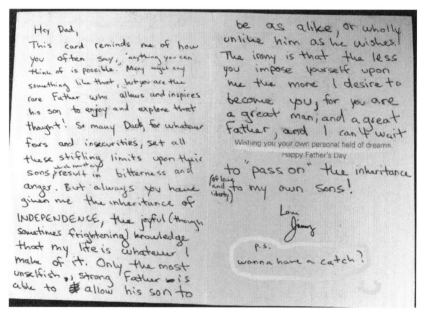

Hey Dad,

This card reminds me of how you often say, "anything you can think of is possible." Many might say something like that, but you are the rare Father who allows and inspires his son to enjoy and explore that thought! So many Dads, for whatever fears and insecurities, set all these stifling limits upon their sons, and most of result in bitterness and anger. But always you have given me the inheritance of INDEPENDENCE, the joyful (though sometimes frightening) knowledge that my life is whatever I make of it. Only the most unselfish, strong Father is able to allow his son to be as alike, or wholly unlike him as he wishes! The irony is that the less you impose yourself upon me the more I desire to become you, for you are a great man, and a great Father, and I can't wait

Wishing you your own personal field of dreams.
Happy Father's Day

to "pass on" the inheritance (of love and liberty) to my own sons!

Love,
Jimmy

p.s.
wanna have a catch?

Casey's 2006 Father's Day card from Jimmy

David Cline hugging a friend

"Your Son, Your Father and You:" Jimmy, Grover Gauntt, Jr., and Casey

Jimmy from the "other side," Zion National Park 2008

Hilary Tedrow Gauntt-Menlo Atherton High School 1968

Jeff Phair with his father, David

Andie Kwasny

Rabbi Regina Sandler-Phillips (photo courtesy of Lise Stern)

Sean Alexander Canepa

Sean Canepa's Messenger

CONDOLENCES: A DIFFICULT DUTY

KNOWING WHAT TO say when a friend, acquaintance, or stranger loses a loved one is never easy, especially when the death came suddenly, unexpectedly. Many will rush to CVS and buy one of those pre-printed Hallmark cards. Maybe they'll hastily scrawl some well-intentioned words and drop it in the post as fast as they can. Other well-meaning folks will shun the task altogether, using myriad excuses: "I don't know what to say." "What if I don't use the right words?" "I didn't write (or call) right away, and now it's too late." "They'll probably think I've been ignoring them because I didn't get in touch as soon as it happened." And perhaps worst of all: "They must think I don't care for not sending a card or calling."

In 2014 I wrote a post: "How to Write a Beautiful Condolence Card to Someone Who Has Lost a Child." We included it in the Appendix to *Suffering Is the Only Honest Work*. It has consistently been the most visited post on WriteMeSomethingBeautiful.com.

I completely get how hard it is. Several years before Jimmy's accident, the four-year-old son of my longtime dentist was tragically killed when a cave he and a friend were digging in their backyard collapsed and he suffocated. What did I do? Found a new dentist. *Mea culpa.*

We received hundreds of sympathy cards and letters, and noticed the ones that really stood head and shoulders above the rest had the following six ingredients:

- Open strong and say something from your heart.
- Compliment the one who is gone.
- Share a favorite memory or connection with the child.
- Compliment the parents (or the siblings).
- Say something uplifting.
- Take your time.

A year later, I wrote a companion post to offer some help to those who are confronted with yet another seemingly impossible task. This is the second most-visited post on our website: "How to Write a Beautiful Condolence Card to Someone Who Has Lost a Loved One to Suicide."

The aftermath of Jimmy's death and my father's suicide could not have been more different. In addition to the tsunami of cards, a steady stream of family, our friends, Jimmy's friends, flowers, and food deliveries poured into our house that first week. A thousand sorrowful souls attended his memorial service, and several friends and family members spoke so beautifully and powerfully in their remembrances of Jimmy.

Upon learning of Dad's death, a few family members flew into Chicago's O'Hare airport. A handful of friends came by the house. About twenty-five mute souls attended his memorial service at the Itasca Presbyterian Church on Christmas Eve day. There were no photos of my father, no casket. Reverend Tom Hinkin was the only one who spoke. The family went back to our house, where we men huddled around a table in our kitchen and drank scotch. There was no wake, no celebration of life. My father's death was not feted.

Suicide makes strangers of neighbors and friends. Family, too. Suicide is crushing, unthinkable, unfathomable, and frightening.

What can you say? What can you do when your initial instinct is to just run? The question—implied and explicit—is why? Why did this happen? Isn't there something more that could have been done? That I could have done?

The fear of those around me, the sheer fact that everyone was so immobilized by the shock of my father's suicide, compounded the fear and anger that welled up in me. I went back to finish my junior year at USC after the "holidays" and told only two of my fraternity brothers what really happened to my dad. To everyone else I lied. "He had a heart attack."

So, when someone you know loses a loved one to suicide, this will not only be the hardest condolence card you write, it may just be the most important. In the "Condolences: Loss of a Child" post, I include several "Don'ts." Here are two additional ones.

- **Don't run away.** Suppress every instinct to the contrary and run to the side of your friend or loved one. Truly, one of the most important and helpful things you can do following a death by suicide is show up with a card, other remembrance or, better yet, a personal visit and a hug.
- **Don't treat this death differently.** The fact is, whether the person was struck by a car at age 24, succumbed to a long illness at the age of 90 (my dear mother), or died by suicide at 51, they have left their bodies and begun the next leg of the journey. How you approach a death by suicide with your friend or loved one will play a role in how they move forward with their life. If you feed the victim aura—either with the words you use or by saying nothing at all—this may stunt their healing process. Those who have lost someone they deeply love, no matter how or when, are not victims. They are survivors. Do unto them as such.

The six ingredients of a beautiful condolence card equally apply to a death by suicide. This is a letter I wrote standing in the shoes of one of my father's best friends, the late Jim Walton. Jim was in charge of the Case Foundation job in Coalwood, and it was he who convinced my dad I should spend the summer there.

Dear Casey,

I am heartbroken over the sudden and tragic loss of your father. Your dad was my best friend. We served together as officers in the Army during World War II, including two years in the South Pacific. He saved my life on more than one occasion, and I did the same for him. Grover is one of the bravest and most courageous men I know. At the end of the war we were stuck in Manila and forced to type up summaries of the many battles our regiment participated in. We finally had enough and took our typewriters and threw them into the ocean. We told our commanding officer they were stolen by locals.

As you know, I worked with your dad for many years at Case Foundation Company, where he continued to display his exceptional leadership and organizational skills. He taught me a lot.

Your dad loved you very much. He was always so proud and bragged to everyone of how well you have done in school and sports and the work ethic you exhibited at such an early age working all those summers at Case. I so enjoyed having the opportunity to be your supervisor that summer we worked on the ventilation shaft project for Olga Coal Company in Coalwood, West Virginia, after you graduated from high school. You worked hard and fit in so well with the folks there.

All of the exceptional qualities I observed in your dad have been passed on to you. You are destined to be successful and a good father when that time comes for you. I regret not being able to attend your dad's service, but I am flying to Los Angeles next week and look forward to our dinner together. Please accept my deepest condolences, Casey.

Sincerely,

Jim Walton

Jim didn't come to my dad's funeral. Neither did he send a card or come see me. The fact is that none of my family ever saw or heard from Jim Walton after Dad's death. But I know, in my heart, he would have written those words to me if only he could have stopped running.

Let's address some of the other questions that come up with condolences.

Is it okay to send a condolence card to someone you don't know?
Hilary was deeply moved by an obituary she read in the *San Diego Union-Tribune* of a woman she didn't know, Joan Smith. She was directed to Legacy.com, should she wish to leave a message for the family.

According to its website, Legacy.com is the global leader in online obituaries and partners with most major newspapers all over the world, so the odds are good that if an obituary is published in a paper and you search the name of that person, you will be directed to his or her memorial page on Legacy.

Hilary posted this in Joan's Guest Book: "This message is for Robert, the loving son of the incredible Joan. I didn't know your mother, but the amazing story you wrote of her life brought me to tears and inspired me. You have honored her in the best way in putting your heart and soul into this announcement of her loss. I am her same age, and have shared this with friends who have also, like me, chosen motherhood. Your deep appreciation for that choice honors us all, and we thank you. I lost a son a decade ago and promise you this grief you must be feeling will soften, and the love you feel will always remain. God Bless your family.

Hilary Gauntt"

When you post a message, you are asked to submit your email address. The public can't see it, but the family members have it in case they would like to correspond. A few days later, Hilary received this message from Robert:

Subject: You're very kind

Hello, Hilary. Thank you for your kind message. It brought me to tears. I always knew that my Mom was a special individual, both for me and for everyone, yet I unfortunately could not appreciate it fully until after she passed.

Robert went on to reflect on birthday, Christmas, and Halloween cards she'd send. He shared memories of waking to her fresh-baked pastries on Saturday mornings and her helping hand in the yard, as well as countless acts he never saw and might never truly appreciate. That, to him, was unconditional love, a type of love only a mother has for her children.

He commiserated with Hilary over losing Jimmy and mentioned that his maternal grandparents lost their firstborn to cancer when he was 11 years old. The only time he saw his grandfather cry was when their son's ashes were interred a second time in San Diego after having been in Detroit. He wrote, *Sixty years later the pain of losing a child was all too real...I am sorry that it was a pain that came to you.*

Robert reflected further on love and loss, and closed,

Thank you, truly, for your very kind email and for, in the process, allowing me some space to share a few additional words.

Wishing you peace and love now and always.

Rob

So, do we think sending your sympathy to a stranger is okay? Yeah, it's more than okay!

Here's another question that plagues many a mind.

When is it too late to send condolences?

I'd venture a guess most folks would tell you that saying something weeks, months, or even years after a person dies is simply taboo. Doing so will only reopen wounds and make the family feel awful. Trust me on this: The exact opposite is true. Hugh Sill and I discovered this with our boys, as we explored in "For Nika." Here's one more of our many testaments to this truth: It's never too late.

I received an email in the early evening on Thursday, November 15, 2018. It arrived a week before Thanksgiving and a week after what would have been Jimmy's 35th birthday. His birthday and holidays are always emotional, and sometimes the metaphysical/spiritual pot gets stirred and stuff happens.

Hilary and I sat in front of the television, more in desultory conversation than watching a less-than-riveting program. Hilary paged through a magazine. My phone buzzed, and I gave it a glance. I had a new email from a Rabbi Regina Sandler-Phillips. The name didn't ring a bell, but the subject line immediately got my attention: YOUR SON…YOUR FATHER…AND YOU.

Rabbi Regina wrote, *You don't know me, but 13 years ago this month I participated in the 2005 Bearing Witness retreat at Auschwitz-Birkenau with your son and brother. I had some wonderful conversations at that retreat with your son (whom I knew as Jim), and from time to time look affectionately at some retreat photos taken by Peter Cunningham.*

My heart was racing and my eyes were getting a little misty on my first high-speed pass through her email.

There were two photos attached. The first one, titled "Jamesx2," showed Jimmy and another James whom I didn't recognize. In it Jimmy smiles slyly at the camera, as if to let the viewer know he has something up his sleeve, or that he has a secret he knows you'd like to be in on. He looks older than 21. Angelic, yet with an all-knowing grin. And he's looking at the camera—at us—not where his friend is looking.

Oh, my God! We had never before seen this photo of Jimmy. It felt like we were receiving, through the rabbi as our medium, a big "Hello!" from Jimmy. Strike "it felt like." I knew in my heart it was without question a message from our son. My body convulsed with shudders and goose bumps. Tears escaped as I choked on sobs.

The television volume muffled my meltdown, and Hilary kept reading. She didn't see my distress and, after a brief internal debate, I decided to hold off sharing this with her and our daughter until the next morning.

I went back to the email for a more careful reading. Rabbi Regina wrote, *I am not on social media and have not been in touch with most fellow retreatants until the past few days, when I put together a blog post on my 2005 experiences at the Bearing Witness Retreat.*

She had recently reconnected with James Powell, the young man with Jimmy in the photo, then looked online for Jimmy. *Only in the last hour did I discover the tragedy with which you and your family have lived every day for the past ten years,* she went on. *Then I read about your personal transformation and healing in two generational directions, and decided to reach out to you.*

She had obviously read our story of my father's letter that arrived at precisely the moment it would have the most impact and meaning for me and our family. I was deeply moved by her words. She doesn't know me. But she got me so right. She would have even more profound observations to share with me over the next couple of years.

Rabbi Regina ended by saying, *I wanted to express my deepest appreciation for your loving, spiritual gifts that shine out of the depths of great pain. May the memories of James Tedrow Gauntt—and your father, Grover Cleveland Gauntt, Jr.—continue to be for many blessings of healing, consolation, hope and peace.*

The second photo showed Jimmy clowning at the celebration on the final night the retreatants spent in Krakow. He's on the staircase, holding the rabbi's hand as she does a backbend. My silver-haired brother, Grover , is visible to the left and behind Regina.

This picture held incredible meaning and memories for me. Though our fun-loving, outgoing son would never have been mistaken for a contemplative, he had joined the Buddhist Club when he was attending USC, perhaps as a nod to my brother, whose compassionate heart has led him to dedicate his life to peace, healing, and helping mankind suffer less.

My brother is a dedicated and accomplished master Zen teacher with a deep understanding and expression of the Dharma, meaning cosmic law and order. Since 1996, Grover has led people from all faiths and many countries in meditations at the Nazi death camps to honor and remember the victims. They call these annual pilgrimages Bearing Witness retreats.

Jimmy spent his 2005–2006 senior year in London attending Queen Mary University. He traveled extensively across Great Britain and Europe at every possible opportunity. When his uncle invited him to join The Zen Peacemaker Organization in Poland for a week to bear witness to Nazi atrocities, Jimmy jumped at the chance.

So in November, uncle and nephew found themselves inside Auschwitz-Birkenau, along with Rabbi Regina and many others from all over the world, sitting in silence in front of the Birkenau crematories. At the end of the week, they had all gathered to celebrate life's victory over death. Here was Jimmy, alive forever in Kodachrome, a gift from a rabbi.

The next morning, I called Brittany and asked her to come over. I showed her and her mother the email and photos from the rabbi. Brittany's reaction to the photo said it best. "That picture of Jimmy! He looks so much like Mom. And just so something. Different. Like Jimmy from the future." Hilary burst into tears—mostly tears of surprise and joy in seeing photos of him she had never seen before. They both just knew, like my first reaction, that Jimmy was clearly saying, "Hi."

We all agreed how wonderful and courageous Rabbi Regina had been to reach out to us 13 years after she met Jimmy that one time.

Not many would bother to offer condolences at such a late date, particularly someone who was a stranger to us.

But then again, she is a rabbi, and after I read more on her website about her and her work, I realized she is a deeply spiritual, compassionate healer, and has devoted much of her life to helping others deal with the challenges and opportunities of life and death.

The more I thought about the rabbi's email, the more something nagged at me. Why was she reaching out to me now, after so many years, at this particular moment in time? Don't get me wrong. I am more than grateful that she did—our whole family is. Then it hit me: James Powell—the other James in the photo.

A few months after Jimmy died, and with my brother's help, I found and reached out to James Powell in London. I didn't know him, but something important happened to Jimmy on that 2005 retreat and it involved James. I needed to talk to him about it and also let him know about Jimmy in case he hadn't heard. I wrote about it in the "Brothers" chapter of *Suffering Is the Only Honest Work.*

I checked my emails—I keep everything involving Jimmy—and discovered my first connection with James Powell was on November 15, 2008. Ten years to the day before Rabbi Regina's email.

Of course it was.

And thanks to her, we now know what James Powell looks like.

꿍

[In the Appendix we address condolences in the midst of the COVID-19 pandemic.]

THE ONES WHO FIND
OUT YEARS LATER

A COUPLE OF weeks after Rabbi Regina reached out to me with those beautiful photos of Jimmy and her belated condolences, the topic of "those-who-just-found-out" came up at a gathering of our Fraternity of Dads. Jeffrey Miller mentioned running into an old friend at a reunion of his medical school class. They hadn't seen each other for many years.

The acquaintance asked Jeffrey, "How is your daughter, Ariana? Didn't she have some issues with her heart?"

Jeffrey's reply drained all of the color from the poor fellow's face. "Ariana passed away ten years ago. She was 13."

Chris Ramirez also became the bearer of bad tidings when he was in Texas over Thanksgiving, visiting his daughter. He ran into an old buddy in a bar in Corpus Christi, a tough ex-Marine with three tours in Afghanistan. Eight years earlier, Chris and his eight-year-old son, Christian, had spent an afternoon with the Marine. They played with his remote-controlled airplane and, as they were getting ready to leave, he gave it to Christian.

After a hug at the bar, his friend asked, "Hey, how's Christian?"

"Oh, man, I'm sorry to have to tell you this. Christian died six years ago."

The tough ex-Marine fell to pieces and was inconsolable.

I remember early on when this would happen—running into an acquaintance or colleague who didn't know—and thinking, "How is this possible? Everyone in the entire Universe must have known Jimmy died. This was a world-ending event!" Now 12 years in, it occurs less frequently, but it's still a bit of a stunner.

Both Jeffrey and Chris observed that with the passing of the years, it's less tough (note the avoidance of the word "easier") to let folks know of their child's passing. However, it remains painful to see the shock, horror, disbelief, and devastation in the eyes of the unsuspecting as they get the news for the first time. It's like looking in a mirror and seeing what our faces must have looked like when we got "the news."

My brothers-in-loss are now at a place where we can actually feel sorry for those-who-just-found-out.

'TIS A FEARFUL THING

IF YOU'VE WATCHED the Netflix series *Godless*, you'll recognize these words from the final scene of the final episode, in which an unknown pastor shows up at the tail end of a funeral. He reads a poem that brings tears to everyone present:

> 'Tis a fearful thing
> to love what death can touch.
> A fearful thing
> to love, to hope, to dream, to be—
> to be,
> And oh, to lose.
> A thing for fools, this,
> And a holy thing,
> a holy thing
> to love.
> For your life has lived in me,
> your laugh once lifted me,
> your word was gift to me.
> To remember this brings painful joy.
> 'Tis a human thing, love,

> a holy thing, to love
> what death has touched.

Although the show and many others mistakenly attribute the poem to Yehuda Halevi (d.1141), it was in fact written in the 20th century by Rabbi Chaim Stern (1930–2001) of Brooklyn, New York.

Life. "A thing for fools, this."

One could easily conclude life is just one elaborate setup for suffering. From the moment we are born, we bond with our parents, our grandparents, our siblings; build close friendships; fall in love; marry; have children of our own—we are destined to endure the pain of losing someone we love over and over again.

And yet, we choose life. Our daughter suffered mightily the loss of her 24-year-old brother and witnessed the devastating body blows thrown at her parents. Two years later she and her husband brought new life into this world, followed by another two years after that.

Why do conscious, highly intelligent beings like us embark on this fool's errand? Is it not insanity to do the same thing over and over again and expect a different result?

We tell ourselves this time we'll bring a new life into this world that death will not touch, which death has proven since life began cannot be true.

So, what is it that makes us choose life?

Rabbi Stern teaches us it's love.

Love, life, death, and love. The circle of our essence—our being—does not change.

Rabbi Stern's closing lines are profound truth and resonate deeply: "It is a human thing, love, a holy thing, to love what death has touched."

Love survives death. Death does not touch love or erase love. Death takes the body—the shell. Love is eternal.

We know this at our deepest core. It is hard-wired into our souls.

But what does that mean, eternal love?

Rabbi Rick Rheins of Denver, a student and protégé of the poet, provided some wonderful insight into Rabbi Stern's poem and the Jewish practices and rituals of Yahrzeits, Yizkors, and Kaddish performed and recited by those who have suffered the death of a loved one.

Rabbi Rheins says funeral and mourning rituals are not magical incantations. They "connect us to spiritual dimensions that we can sense, but not define. We can almost feel the presence of our loved ones bound gently with us."

The rabbi observes that for some, acknowledging that ongoing connection may be upsetting or painful, so they try to avoid it. They don't perform the rituals; they don't go to synagogue or church. They view death as a wall separating them from their loved ones. They think death touches love, and if they hide from their loss they will be protected against greater suffering.

I readily admit I was one of the "deniers" and "hiders" after my father's death. I walled off his memory, his love for me, in the futile belief and attempt that would shield me from the pain.

Rabbi Rheins says the act of performing the rituals and reciting the prayers "strengthen the spiritual essence of those who have passed and those yet to be born, bringing us the gift of heavenly peace." Think about that. We are already connected to *those who have yet to be born.* That's heavy stuff and will require some more musing.

Despite the specter of inevitable loss, we choose to bring new life into being, to commit to love, because on some plane we know and trust that the connection can never be severed. It is our soul's connection between "this side" and "the other side."

Yes, death is painful, it hurts, but our love endures. Our loved ones remain close to us, connected to us. Our relationships with our loved ones not only continue, they can be strengthened. If broken, they can be mended and repaired. Love is a *holy thing*. It's bigger than us, separate from our body. Love not only survives, but it transcends and takes us (and those pieces of us that split off) with it for glimpses into a spiritual dimension. Glimpses of heaven here on earth.

That dimension is accessible to us and to our loved ones. As Monsignor Clement Connolly observed earlier, "There is a world beyond our knowing—in rare and sacred moments it is revealed to us. There God dwells. From that place of mystery our loved ones are ever present to us. It takes pensive moments, a convergence of unexpected miracles and then the eyes of faith to see and feel and experience it."

There are many ways to access this spiritual dimension, this other world, and connect with our loved ones, those who have already transitioned and those waiting for their opportunity to come here. Reciting prayers and performing rituals at places of worship is certainly one of them. For others, meditation is a pathway. Writing is my portal.

IF YOU WRITE IT, THEY WILL COME

My Sanctuary in the Wilderness

A FEW YEARS back my muse and brother-in-loss, George Blystone, sent me a reaction to one of our posts of inexplicable synchronicities: "I have no doubt that the laws of probability will continue to be irrelevant as you continue to encounter people who are desperately in need of hope and reasons to believe. Perhaps it is the literary *Field of Dreams*: If you write it, they will come. Maybe your reward is a catch with Jimmy and your Dad."

Of course, George could not know his mention of the 1989 movie *Field of Dreams* would bring me to my knees, crying dinosaur tears. It's impossible for me to count the hours Jimmy and I spent in our yard playing catch through the joyful and stressful years of T-ball, Little League, Pop Warner, and high school football. He threw righty, although he was a natural lefty. He worked it out.

Blystone didn't know our family was bewitched by Kevin Costner's film and Jimmy's and my "thing" about the signature scene. The Costner character's father, who had a "cup of coffee" in big league baseball, and has been dead for years, comes out of the cornfields and walks on his son's newly constructed baseball field on his farm in the middle of Iowa. Costner says, "Dad, you want to have a catch?" I cry every time they start throwing the ball to each other.

When Jimmy got older and came home for visits from college, we had a standing joke. When discussing plans, rather than using the direct approach, "Hey, what do you want to do?" Jimmy or I would ask, "Wanna have a catch?" We'd have a good laugh and then go boogie boarding, play tennis, or golf.

That was our thing. Although he didn't—couldn't—know the background of all this, instinctively, intuitively, George had tapped into something truly profound. That is the essence of the depth of my friendship with this guy—he gets me.

If you write it, they will come.

I wrote a post for our website awhile back titled "A Place I Go—My Sanctuary." I included a short impromptu piece I did for a writing class I took from Judy Reeves at UCSD back in 2010. I thought at the time I must be a little crazy to write and share with my classmates about falling into wormholes, traveling with spirit guides, walking through walls of water, and meeting up and talking with Jimmy and my dad. They thought I made it all up.

But you see, writing is my conduit, my wormhole that connects me with our son—and my father and other family members, some of whom, like Aunt Mary, are many generations removed and I've never met, at least in this lifetime.

As we touched upon in "Heal," Dr. Alan Wolfelt, in his wonderful book *Companioning the Bereaved,* says our grief journey requires us to spend time in the wilderness, to find a place of solitude where we can empty ourselves, and begin to become refilled. His definition of "sanctuary" deeply resonates with me: "A place of refuge from external demands. A space where the mourner is free to disengage from the outside world. A place where the need to turn inward and suspend will not be hurried or ridiculed."

Writing is my sanctuary. Writing is how and where I access the spiritual dimension of my grief and, somehow, it can access me.

Writing is how I probe my deepest feelings, thoughts, and questions, my deeper self. It's how I stick my head into the rabbit hole. When I go into my sanctuary and write it's like getting on a plane, or more aptly a spaceship, that takes me to places I never before imagined.

Even more than the words it is the act of writing that helps me organize my thoughts, project them out into the Universe, and occasionally tap into the mysteries and wonders all around us. We've been extraordinarily rewarded with the many pingbacks we've received. Think Jodie Foster in the film *Contact*.

Because of writing, I've made deep, profound connections with many, many wonderful people I otherwise never would have met. Together, we've plumbed the depths of sorrow, pain, and suffering, and the soaring heights and infinite power of love everlasting.

In my sanctuary I've repaired and forged stronger, more loving relationships with my family and friends.

My sanctuary is the antithesis of lonely.

Mary Wisniewski wrote an article for the *Chicago Tribune* titled "When You Write, You're Right," extolling the many benefits of journaling. Here are a few.

Psychologists who recommend that patients keep journals say writing can be a way of relieving stress, moving past trauma, firing creativity, and giving life meaning.

Journaling allows you to tap into the unconscious, which opens a door to creativity.

Ms. Wisniewski is quick to point out that posting on social media is not journaling. "People on social media tend to put on a happy face. In journal writing, people have an opportunity to face their vulnerability and whatever imperfections that they may be struggling with and be real with that."

Susan Hannifin-MacNab, in her book *A to Z Healing Toolbox*, devotes an entire chapter, "J," to the Healing Power of Journaling. She emphasizes there are different ways to journal and recommends finding the one most comfortable for you.

Susan writes, "The act of transferring conscious or subconscious words, feelings, and images from mind to paper may help to release internal feelings of despair, promote a sense of self-compassion, and provide a stepping stone to realize future hopes, goals, and dreams."

I began to journal a couple of weeks after Jimmy died. I continue to journal, although with less frequency since I've been doing more blogging. However, I always journal my vivid dreams, the ones that seem to come in the early morning before I wake up. I handwrite my dream recollections. I do that because it's more personal, and it enables me to go slow and dig deeper into the nuances of the dream.

And sometimes when I do that, I can get back into the dream and more spills out. ... I also journal my vivid dreams because mine are so elusive. If I don't write them down right away, I forget them. They're gone.

When I go back and reread what I wrote about one of those dreams, I have no recollection of ever having that dream. It's like I'm experiencing it for the first time. That's why I refer to my journal as my "dream catcher." Hilary and I also have actual dream catchers hanging from our nightstands. You can't be too prepared.

When Steve Date was putting together his film *The Letter*, I sent him several photos and some reels of old Super 8 film from the late 1960s. One of the film clips he used was shot in the summer of 1969, of my dad and me playing catch with a tennis ball.

Before my dad's letter arrived, I couldn't watch that clip without a shadow of gloom enveloping me. Now, there he is, vibrant, barefoot, in yellow Bermuda shorts and a white short-sleeved dress shirt, fit, a huge grin on his face, winging the ball to me, finishing off with a high kick. That is how I now choose to remember my dad: having a catch in our backyard with big smiles on our faces.

My dad died 18 months later.

That's why George brought me to tears.

Because he is absolutely right.

If you write it, they will come.

And I would also add, with my father's letter as Exhibit A:

If they write it, they will come.

Oh, and one more thing George didn't know about—the Father's Day card Jimmy gave to me in 2006. The cover is a photo of a man stretched out on his back in the middle of a golden field, his glasses and newpaper resting on the front of his dress shirt and necktie. A butterfly is perched on the toe of one of his wingtipped shoes. You don't see the man's head. I have the impression he's asleep.

The printed message inside the card reads: **Wishing you your own personal field of dreams.**

Jimmy also handwrote this long, loving message on the inside of the card:

Hey Dad, This card reminds me of how you often say "anything you can think of is possible." Many might say something like that, but you are the rare Father who allows and inspires his son to enjoy and explore that thought! So many Dads, for whatever fears and insecurities, set all these stifling limits upon their sons which must only result in bitterness and anger. But always you have given me the inheritance of INDEPENDENCE, the joyful (though sometimes frightening) knowledge that my life is whatever I make of it. Only the most unselfish, strong Father is able to allow his son to be as alike, or wholly unlike him as he wishes. The irony is that the less you impose yourself upon me the more I desire to become you, for you are a great man and a great Father, and I can't wait to pass on the inheritance of love and liberty to my own sons! Love Jimmy

p.s. wanna have a catch?

Oh, son, do I ever.

It's a holy thing to love what death has touched.

THOSE SIGNS THEY SEND

And when I say give something to the world, I don't mean accomplishments in the conventional sense. I mean just making life just that much better for the people around you. Live your life. It's the only thing worth living for.

—David Cline

THIS STORY CAME to me from our dear friends Kimberly Higgins and her younger sister, Kerry Cline.

Kerry began working as a nursing staffer at Santa Monica Hospital in 2010. Recently, she was offered a significant promotion to the position as head of Nursing Staffing at UCLA Medical Center's Santa Monica Hospital and Ronald Reagan Hospital in Westwood. In this role she would oversee the 13 staffers for both hospitals and be responsible for making sure the patients in the 780 beds are served by the precise number of nurses mandated by law and within the center's budget.

Kerry joked with her sister Kim, "After all the years of being a subordinate, I can't really imagine being an 'ordinate.'" She was simultaneously thrilled to be deemed worthy and terrified of the enormous responsibilities and expectations the job entailed. She needed time to decide whether or not to accept the promotion.

She also felt taking the position would be a betrayal of her youngest son, David. What right did she have to be excited, to start what amounted to a new life, only three years after David had gone?

In late 2016, David Cline, along with 35 others, tragically died in the Ghost Ship fire in Oakland. An old two-story warehouse had been illegally converted into live/workspaces for artists and used as an occasional music venue. That night the Ghost Ship, as it was then known, hosted an electronic music gathering. A fire broke out just before midnight. The building was instantly engulfed in flames, and 36 of the 100 or so concert-goers were not able to escape the building.

A 2014 graduate of UC Berkeley, David was only 24. At Santa Monica High School, he helped his volleyball team win the California CIF championship. His passion for music led him to become a virtuoso on the clarinet he'd played since second grade. The energy and creativity of electronic music intrigued him. Everyone loved David.

This was not Kerry's and her husband, Denny's, first walk into this dark valley. In 1986, Denny was attending law school at Cal Berkeley when they welcomed their firstborn. The life-changing joy and wonder they experienced during that first month of new life plummeted into grief when their healthy newborn son, Riley Marsden, died of SIDS (sudden infant death syndrome) the night he turned four weeks old.

Kerry and Denny picked themselves up and would bring into this world three more strapping boys: Kenny, Neil, and the "baby," David.

The loss of one child is unimaginable. Two—there are no words. Kerry took a leave of absence from her job when David died and, after several months, wanted to return to work. However, nurse staffing would be challenging and stressful, and her grief continued to sap her energy and ability to focus. Her superiors offered her what she called the "deliciously subordinate" job of administrative assistant to various nursing supervisors. A couple of years later, one of Kerry's superiors encouraged her to apply for the position of head of Nursing Staffing.

Grief is complex, becoming part of our precious connection to the one we've loved so hard and lost too soon. While we understand on a head level, at the heart level anxiety at the prospect of it easing or taking another form seems disloyal to the ones we miss so much. With the offer of the promotion in hand, Kerry was at that crossroads.

When the day came for her to announce her decision, Kerry felt she was at a breaking point. What would David think of her moving on?

And then three things happened.

As Kerry walked out of their house in Santa Monica to go to work, she was greeted by the most beautiful sunrise she'd ever seen. Then, as she unlocked the car door, she dropped her keys. Lying next to the keys was a beautiful white feather.

Kerry knew in the depths of her soul that the sunrise and feather were clear messages from David.

When she got to her office, she began to clear out her desk. Whatever she decided, she'd be moving to another office.

Then the third message appeared in the bottom of a drawer. She found an article that one of her colleagues had given her soon after David died. Kerry didn't remember reading it. If she had, she wasn't in a place to be able to absorb the words.

On the first page of the article was a painting of a woman dreaming of a young boy, and it compelled Kerry to sit down and start reading. It was instantly obvious this was written by a mother who had lost her son three years before the article appeared. Daniel,

22 years old and a recent graduate of Stanford University, died of NORSE, a rare seizure disorder that inexplicably strikes healthy people with no history of epilepsy.

This mother's grief was as raw as Kerry's. Words leapt from the pages. She had written, "I violated the basic canon of motherhood. I failed to protect my child. That my child is dead while I still live defies the natural order.

"I love my husband and our two surviving children, but I couldn't transfer my love for Daniel to them. It was for him alone… my love for Daniel bruised me."

One day the mother cried out to Daniel in desperation. "What will I do with my love for you, Daniel?" Closing her eyes, she suddenly saw Daniel standing there.

He spoke. "Just love me, Mom."

"But where are you?" she asked.

His frustration was palpable as he said, "I'm here!" And then he was gone.

Daniel's mother wept as release swept over her. She could continue to love him, only in a new way. For the rest of her life she would carry this son, forever 22, and others who knew him would also carry him whenever they looked out at the world with compassion, when they acted with determination and kindness, when they were brave enough to contemplate all the things in life that remain unknown.

The article closed with, "I will search for Daniel, but without desperation. I look for him in others. My search is lifted by his words: *Just love me, Mom. I'm here!*"

In that instant Kerry felt David encouraging her to accept the promotion by giving her the sunrise, the feather, and this article. She was not letting David down. She wouldn't love him any less. He would be happy that she could move forward and do even more good work helping others.

Kerry took another quick look at the first page of the article and noticed for the first time the date: December 2, 2016. The same day her David had ascended to heaven.

Kerry picked up the phone and called the Medical Center's administrator.

"I accept."

She has been head of Nursing Staffing ever since.

Postscript

The article Kerry found in her desk was written by Dr. Nora Wong and appeared in the *New York Times*. Dr. Wong is now the executive director of The NORSE Institute, whose mission is to find a cure for the disease that claimed the life of her son, Daniel. I recently reached out and sent her Kerry's story. I thought she should know how her heartfelt article dramatically impacted the life and choice of another grieving mom. Dr. Wong replied the same day:

"I am so sorry to learn of the tragic deaths of David and Riley, and of your son, Jimmy. I am always amazed at the magical connections and messages provided by our loved ones who are no longer on earth. I'm so glad my article played a small, positive role in Kerry's decision to embark on a new journey in life. Please let Kerry and her sister Kimberly know that there is another coincidence. When Daniel was in the ICU for seventy-nine days, his bedside nurses were the ones who sustained us. We are still in contact with them. As head of Nursing Staffing, Kerry is helping terrified parents like my husband and me."

So, indeed, tragedy can be turned into something compassionate and good.

Especially when we accept the help from our loved ones on the other side.

YOUR SON, YOUR FATHER, AND YOU

IN ADDITION TO sending those amazing photos of Jimmy and her beautiful words of condolence, Rabbi Regina shared some profoundly deep and prescient observations regarding the story—the miracle—of the letter from my father:

"As we accept and find meaning in the wounds we may always carry with us through this precious life, whenever death comes, whether suddenly and tragically or in the fullness of time, we and our relationships can heal beyond our bodies and lifetimes, even when no 'cure' is available.

"There is a parallel process for the healing of relationships. Even traumatic death can yield into a healing of relationships through generations: Your son, your father and you."

We and so many others who have lost those they deeply love have experienced the many mind-bending ways they help us from the other side. We are in awe and wonder of how they are able to get messages to us, appear to us as Christian did in the hospital, visiting his grandfather; as Jimmy did for his mother and aunt in front of the Café Les Deux Magots in Paris; as Ben did, having died only a few hours earlier, showing up at the hospital in Chicago to help his close friend John over to the other side; as Nick did, through the gifts he left for his parents after he was killed in a terrorist attack.

In "Healing All Around," Jimmy showed up at his "big bro's" wedding to not only deliver his toast, but more importantly help his friends in attendance, all of whom had been struggling mightily over his death the previous nine years. And, in particular, Henry, the last person to see him alive.

As we shared in "Want to Go for a Ride?" in *Suffering*, Jimmy orchestrated that massive synchronicity to help me reconnect with George Blystone and many other childhood friends I had abandoned 40 years earlier. Their enduring friendship and love for me was enormously helpful to my healing. And I in turn was able to help some of those friends, including George, who would lose children within a few years after our reconnection.

And, of course, there's the letter from my father, when his words of confession, fatherly advice, and eternal love consoled me on Jimmy's 25th birthday. On that same day, Jimmy did damn near the identical thing for his big sister, Brittany. Ryan, her husband of one year, randomly pulled a book off a shelf and tossed it to Britt. Inside was the birthday card Jimmy had sent to Brittany on her 25th birthday. He signed it *I love you eternally, Jimmy.*

I could go on, but I think you get the picture.

Our loved ones want us to survive and get through and beyond the agonizing pain of their deaths and those holes in our hearts. They know we are hurting. They want to help us with our healing and go to great lengths to make that happen.

And as we progress with our healing, hopefully we get to a place where we can begin to help others who have suffered crushing loss: friends, family, colleagues at work, and even those we don't know.

But Rabbi Regina pointed out something even more profound, an entirely different level of healing. *There is a parallel process for the healing of relationships. Even traumatic death can yield into a healing of relationships through generations.*

This is super-powerful stuff. Not only can our loved ones continue to connect, communicate, and work to help us survivors—parents, siblings, friends—with our healing even after they've discarded their physical bodies, but we, in turn, can help them with their healing, easing their regrets, guilt, remorse for pain they may have caused us, things said or unsaid, goals not completed, and the like.

There are many in our tribe of bereaved parents who have lost loved ones to drug overdoses, suicide, and other traumatic or sudden causes. Some regret that the relationships with their children were broken and can never be repaired.

As we explored in "'Tis a Fearful Thing," death does not touch love. Our relationships with our loved ones do not end with their deaths. We may think there is nothing more we or they can do about those relationships, but that simply is not the case. I would suggest that not only are there things we can do to repair and strengthen the relationships with our loved ones, we need to do them as part of the healing process for ourselves and them.

Rather than slamming it shut, death opens a door, a pathway for us to heal and repair broken relationships or strengthen good ones with our departed loved ones across multiple generations. That pathway is accessible from both ends of the wormhole and always available.

But it is our choice if we want to stick our heads in there.

Tom Zuba eloquently wrote about this in "The Relationship Continues" chapter of *Permission to Mourn*:

"What if I told you
That you will always have a relationship
With the people you love who have died?

And what if I told you that the choice is yours?

You define the relationship.

You are either moving closer
to the people you love who have died,
Or you are pushing them away.
By building a wall."

The wall I'd erected to protect myself from my father, his memory, and his abandonment of me and his family, began to come down when his letter miraculously arrived. In its place appeared a path for me to begin to grieve and heal from his death.

Jimmy's death opened a door, a wormhole, a track, something for my father to travel through and help me in my moment of greatest need.

Before I received the letter, my mother, siblings, and I *never* talked together about Dad's suicide or our respective struggles and coping mechanisms. And I never spoke about him with Brittany and Jimmy.

Jimmy's death and my dad showing up for me when he did was the first step to rebuilding my relationship with him, a relationship I was convinced was forever obliterated. As explained in "Healing with History," I was compelled to learn more about my dad. I widely shared the stories of his early years and "The Letter" with family, friends, people I just met, and on our website.

My search for my dad led me to do something I never dreamed I would do before Jimmy died. I wrote a couple of long letters to my dad and expressed my gratitude for his heroic service during the war and my pride in being his son. I shared my sadness for him and forgave him for leaving us so abruptly. I wrote of my absolute awe at all the strings he had to pull to get his letter to me on the day of Jimmy's birthday. And most of all, my immense gratitude to him for coming to Jimmy's side and helping him over.

I began to have good dreams about my dad instead of the earlier creepy ones where he would just show up at our house in Itasca, preoccupied with something he was working on, and never utter a word. In these new dreams, we talk, laugh, and hug.

I believed I was helping my dad and he was feeling better as well. But how could I really know for sure?

WHEN THE VEIL COMES DOWN

IN EARLY 2020, I had a mediumship phone reading with Chris Lynn, a 70th birthday present from Hilary. Hilary, Brittany, and I think very highly of Chris, aka The Blue Jean Mystic, and her gifts. We've each had other spiritual guidance readings with her: past-lives regression; meet your spirit guides; clearing out any blockages.

But this was my first reading with Chris as a medium and the first mediumship reading I've done without Hilary and Brittany.

Jimmy came through first—he always comes through in our readings.

Chris said, "Jimmy is waving a microphone. He says, 'Dad, it's time to do more talks and speaking to larger gatherings. You'll need a microphone and loudspeakers.'"

She continued, "Jimmy says there's a female that will help you with this speaking project, someone close to your age. Do you know anyone like this?" I thought for a few moments.

"Well, there are Elizabeth Boisson and Irene Vouvalides with Helping Parents Heal." Elizabeth co-founded the grief support group in 2009 shortly after her son, Morgan, died from severe altitude sickness while on a student trip to the base camp of Mt. Everest.

Irene became involved after her daughter and only child, Carly, died from a long battle with esophageal-gastric cancer in 2013.

I told Chris that Helping Parents Heal (HPH) has a huge online presence with over 16,000 members and, from time to time, I've posted some of our stories on their Facebook page. I also mentioned Irene is in charge of the HPH annual conference and speaking programs. "And she's a bit younger, but around my age."

Chris paused the reading. "I'm going to do a vibration test on Helping Parents Heal." I have no idea what that means or how she does it. After a few seconds she said, "I'm getting a 90 percent reading in favor of Helping Parents Heal. You need to reach out to Irene. Jimmy fully supports this."

My great-aunt, Mary Sawyers Cook, came through next. Chris said, "She's saying, 'I had such a good life, a full life. Thank you for shining the light upon my story.'"

I thought that it was very nice of Aunt Mary to acknowledge my efforts. Then Chris said, "Mary is showing me a book and three fingers. She's saying, 'You need to write books with three branches: how connecting with our past helps us with healing here; how we here can deal with the present, the pain, and life's challenges; and how we can lean on and get help from our loved ones on the other side.'"

That was eerily specific and prescient.

Chris moved on. "I feel like I've got a father figure here. He's nodding. Sitting here with us and nodding in understanding and appreciation."

I sucked in my breath. It was Dad! I felt him. I had that same electric, tingly feeling during my first call with Emily Sue Buckberry when she told me she had found and kept his letter, and then five days later when I sat down in our kitchen, holding the still-pristine pages, and read his words to me. We've had many readings over the last 12 years and my dad had never before come through.

Chris went on. "He's saying, 'I've come so far—so far. Thank you for putting the pieces back for me. Because you healed me over here.'"

I choked as I stammered, "That's my dad."

Chris cleared her throat, her own tears welling. "He's so grateful."

Tears poured down my face as I replied, "I was honored to do it."

Chris's voice spiked with sudden revelation as she said to me, "What you and we are doing on this side of the veil has an impact on them, too. That's stunning, and I didn't know that...I didn't know that. I thought they had helpers on their side to help them with whatever they might need. But your father is saying what we do on this side can help them. A continuum. That's the word he wants to use. A continuum."

At this point I was a slobbering wreck. "It works both ways big time. My dad helped me with his letter, and then it was my turn to help him."

Through Chris, Dad acknowledged my help and told me how he felt so grateful and so connected. "He's touching his heart and saying, 'I have my heart back. My heart, it's back.'"

Then Dad referred to his death. "It was a lot for you to have to go through, dealing with my choice."

Chris added, "He thanks you for not damning him in the process. He's so grateful. He just keeps saying, 'So grateful.'"

It's not often you stump the medium, but Dad had.

For my father to come through like this—to acknowledge my work, my efforts to mend our relationship, to bring him back into my life, our family's lives—to help *him* put his pieces back together—reclaim his heart...for him to confirm that, yes, healing and mending relationships works both ways!

I was blown away. Later, when I told Hilary about the session, she wisely observed, "You've come full circle with your father."

So true. I went from wanting absolutely nothing to do with him after his death to where I now feel closer to him and love him more than at any other point in my life. I want to talk about him, brag about him, tell my grandsons about him. Tell the world.

Chris wasn't finished. "We don't always see this connection and the matrix that is formed unless we're looking. Those on the other side are all part of that web, and when one of us on this side—like you—becomes included in the web, it strengthens everything on this side and the other side of the veil.

"'We're becoming whole' is the message your loved ones want to bring forward in unison. 'Even though it doesn't look like it on your side, we are becoming whole. And the human race is becoming whole.'

"Your loved ones are saying, 'The honor is ours. We feel honored when you and others like you are doing this work, this heavy lifting.'"

Chris said she was infused with this incredible feeling and had some difficulty expressing it. Finally she said, "Our words are inadequate, but what they're showing me is there will be a time when there will be no veil. There will be no separation. It's not a case of being on one side of the veil or the other, and when that dissolves—when the veil comes down, that is where heaven will be. There will be utter unity."

Or as Father O'Malley predicted, "The Kingdom is here."

Wow. It's impossible for me to get my tiny brain around the idea, the visual, of the veil coming down and our side and the other side becoming one. Being reunited with Jimmy, my parents, ancestors, and all of those we thought separated from us by generations of lifetimes. Those yet to be born. And that it could possibly happen sooner than we think is simply mind-bending.

My father's and loved ones' words of confirmation showed me in no uncertain terms that helping those on the other side with their healing—mending and strengthening our relationships with them—is a critical key to dissolving the veil.

It is also very important that we help others, here, with their healing, and mend and reestablish relationships with friends and family.

As is establishing relationships and bonding with our ancestors. As Mary has made crystal clear, even though she may have shed her body 90 years ago, she continues to pull strings, tap on shoulders, and connect with us on this side. Having spent so much time discovering her story, I feel as strong a bond with Aunt Mary as if she had never left her body. I feel her right here with me whispering into my ear. By the way, during the reading with Chris, Mary said she wants her story made into a movie. She was most insistent about it.

Initially, I thought my writing about grief and healing and my writing and sharing the stories about my family and ancestors were two separate things. They are not. They are entwined, entangled, and focused on this unifying objective of deeply connecting with those of us here, in our bodies, remaining connected with our loved ones who have transitioned, and forging relationships with those we presumed are inaccessible to us because of the separation of a few or more lifetimes.

If we acknowledge their messages and visits, express our gratitude for them reaching through to us, and we in turn act on those shoulder taps and reach across and pull them closer to us here, the veil becomes thinner and thinner. If we can just surrender to the fact that the only thing separating us from our loved ones on the other side is our stubborn adherence to the notion that death touches love, and our inability or unwillingness to see all of the light around us.

We bereaved, especially during those first tough years, are preoccupied with receiving help from our loved ones. We ask, "Are they okay? Where are they? What are they doing?" We're desperate for a message, any sign that lets us know they aren't lost to us. And our loved ones are more than willing to oblige.

The late, esteemed British writer C.S. Lewis said this in a beautiful condolence letter he wrote to the widow of one of his best friends and fellow writer, Charles Williams:

"I feel my friendship with Charles is not ended. His death has had the very unexpected effect of making death itself look quite different. I believe in the next life ten times more strongly than I did. At moments it seems almost tangible. Reverend Dyson, on the day of the funeral, summed up what many of us felt, 'It is not blasphemous,' he said 'to believe that what was true of Our Lord is, in its less degree, true of all who are in Him. They go away in order to be with us in a new way, even closer than before.'

"A month ago, I would have called this silly sentiment. Now I know better. Charles seems, in some indefinable way, to be all around us now. I do not doubt he is doing and will do for us all sorts of things he could not have done while in the body."

I, too, thought that to be utter nonsense—no, flat impossible—after Jimmy was accidentally struck and killed. He was gone, just like my father, and never coming back, leaving us with our pain, our grief, and holes in our hearts never to be filled. Their deaths put an abrupt end to my relationships with them. Only memories remained and, in the case of my father, nightmares of a relationship so broken by his suicide that I ran as fast and far as I could from him.

Now I know better. First my father, soon followed by Jimmy, have gone to great lengths, *in some indefinable way, to be all around us now.* The incredible miracles experienced by Chris Ramirez, Conrad and Paola, and so many other Shining Light Parents are testaments that those we deeply love *go away in order to be with us in a new way, even closer than before.*

As C.S. Lewis observed, *They* are *doing for us all sorts of things they could not have done while in the body.*

Us. I believe Mr. Lewis carefully chose that word. They are *doing all sorts of things* for not just you or me, but for *us.*

For the parents, the widows, the siblings, other family members, friends and, yes, folks you/they have not met. For those yet to be born. For those who transitioned generations and lifetimes ago.

The collective Universe of *Us*. You don't really believe they expend all that energy and creativity for just a few near and dear, do you? Their messages, contacts, appearances, interactions, and intricately constructed synchronicities are meant to be shared with and by all of *Us*.

Sharing is how we express our gratitude and appreciation for *all they are doing for Us*. It's the cosmic high-five, fist bump, fanny slap. Sharing is one way we can help others here with their healing.

Don't get me wrong. It's absolutely wonderful all of the help we receive from our loved ones. But we can become so focused on our needs that we don't think to ask, "How can we help them? How can we help our loved ones on the other side with their healing? What do they need from us who are here?"

Some might ask, "Why do we need to help those who have passed over? Aren't they in a good place, in Heaven, with God?" Or as Chris Lynn admitted, "I thought they had helpers on their side to help them with whatever they might need."

I'm not so sure about that. The late Ram Dass wrote an essay in 2010 titled "Dying is Absolutely Safe." He observed, "These bodies we live in, and the ego that identifies with it, are just like the old family car. They are functional entities in which our Soul travels through our incarnation. But when they are used up, they die.

"Through it all, who we are is Soul, and when the body and the ego are gone, the Soul will live on, because the Soul is eternal. Eventually, in some incarnation, when we've finished our work, our Soul can merge back into the One, back into God, back into the Infinite. In the meantime, our Soul is using bodies, egos, and personalities to work through the karma of each incarnation."

Or as Jimmy wrote in his "Suffering" poem, "And this death not even a trailhead in the endless loop through ourselves."

I believe my father is one of those "in the meantime." He has more work to do through more incarnations. Jimmy? Maybe not. He was an old soul and my sense is he'd already made several laps around the track. When he blessed us with his rebirth, I think Jimmy was well on his way to One.

If I can help my dad, help him put his pieces back together, help him find his heart, mend our relationship, then that lightens his load and enables him to move on, move forward, and get on to what he needs to learn next. My dad was stuck and we helped push his car out of the snowdrift. Now, instead of focusing on me and his family, he can get back to work on his own evolution.

And just imagine what can happen if more of us help our loved ones on the other side, bring them closer to this side of the veil, closer to One.

If a critical mass of us truly accepts and acknowledges that those we deeply love are all around us and even closer than before.

If we, in turn, reciprocate with mindful expressions of our eternal love, and intentionally work at mending, healing, and strengthening our relationships with them, and help them with their healing.

If we do this across multiple generations of loved ones and ancestors.

With a deep knowing in our hearts that they, too, hear us, feel us, and are so grateful for all the things we are doing for them even though they are no longer in their bodies.

That is when the veil comes down.

I may not see it in this lifetime. But I think I'm also "in the meantime," so maybe in one of my next lives.

I have no idea what it will be like—amazing for sure—but my dad gave me a peek.

A few days after my reading with Chris, I had a dream about my dad. Maria, our housekeeper, came into my home office and said, "There are two men at the door for you."

I went to the front door and there were Dad and Jim Walton,

his best friend since World War II, and whom I introduced in "Condolences."

Even though they served in the Army as majors, now they were decked out in Navy dress whites, holding their hats. Both were trim, tan, and fit, and appeared to be in their 40s. Both wore big smiles in addition to their admirals' clusters.

Bear hugs all around, first with Jim, then my dad, the kind that say, "It's been way too long since the last one." I can still feel the strength in their arms and the scratch of their whiskers on my face as I write this.

I invited them inside and we talked a bit. Dad said he was on leave and had come to tell me we'd be going on vacation together.

"So where is your next assignment after we get back?" I asked.

"Right here with you," he replied.

When the veil comes down.

Jimmy and Dad, I love you eternally.

Want to have a catch?

Postscript

I didn't reach out to Irene Vouvalides at Helping Parents Heal (HPH), as Chris Lynn and Jimmy instructed. Instead, Irene reached out to me four months later and invited me to speak to the Helping Parents Heal community on a Zoom call in July. My talk was recorded, put up on the HPH YouTube Channel, and has been viewed by many. That led to an invitation to speak to their affiliate group, Helping Fathers Heal, in September. And in October, at Irene's urging, the highly regarded evidential medium Suzanne Giesemann invited me to come on her very popular national radio show, *Messages of Hope*.

I'm expecting a call from a movie producer begging to do Mary's story.

Why wouldn't I?

THE CHOICE WE MAKE

Everything can be taken from a man but one thing: the last of the human freedoms—to choose one's attitude to any given set of circumstances, to choose one's own way.

—Viktor E. Frankl,
Man's Search for Meaning

AUSTRIAN PSYCHIATRIST VIKTOR Frankl spent almost four years in Nazi concentration camps during World War II. In his enormously powerful book *Man's Search for Meaning,* Frankl vividly recounts the horrific atrocities inflicted upon him and his fellow prisoners by their captors. Many of the prisoners who were exterminated or slowly succumbed to disease, famine, exposure, and exhaustion had no choice as to their fate.

Frankl chose to live, to do whatever it took to stay alive. Although his first wife and most of his family died in the camps, Frankl remarried, raised a family, wrote over 30 books, and achieved worldwide acclaim as one of the preeminent psychiatrists of his time.

As horrific as Frankl's experiences and suffering were, he chose to continue to live, learn, teach, and love. It's a choice each of us has to make after a tragedy. Here are some of the people that I've been fortunate to meet who have chosen to become stronger and to help others in similar situations.

I first met Patty Reis in 2016. Her loss was a very, very public one. In the early hours of January 1, 2012, her son David, 25, a Navy fighter pilot in the Top Gun training school in San Diego, and her daughter Karen, 24, a University of California at San Diego grad and volleyball player, were murdered in David's apartment in Coronado by his roommate, also a Top Gun pilot, who then died by suicide. National news.

Within a few months Patty returned to her career in Bakersfield as a lactation consultant, helping mothers of newborns with the challenges of breastfeeding. Patti says her work is both life affirming and heartbreaking. "I'm surrounded by new life. It's confusing at times. The moms get to take their children home. Two of mine are dead."

Within a couple of years, Patty was leading two groups of mothers who had lost children. She said, "I became a magnet for moms who experienced loss. The work is cathartic and educational for me." The mothers refer to Patty as their rock.

Patty has studied under Dr. Alan Wolfelt at his Center for Loss & Life Transition, and she is now a certified grief companion. "I cannot say enough positive things about her," he says. "The moms in her groups know she has been where they are now. She walks the walk, and they know it."

Patty helped Nika Sill Morse with breastfeeding her first child, and Nika gave her a copy of our *Suffering* book. We connected soon after.

At our first lunch I asked Patty, "How did you survive that?"

She held my eyes firmly with her own. "We still have two younger children, and I had to be there for them. They were suffering as much if not more than us parents. I couldn't let them down."

Parents like Patty and the Leslies could have chosen to stay in bed, lock themselves in their house, shut everyone and everything out, make friends with alcohol and drugs, and raise a middle finger to God, the Universe, life.

I suspect many of their friends and colleagues would have totally understood that choice and given them a pass. I dare say most probably expected it. Yet, they've chosen to live.

Some don't. As mentioned in "For Nika," in the summer of 1972 I picked pineapples in fields that are now the Kapalua Resort on Maui. That's where I met and befriended John Morehouse. Halfway into the summer John got the heartbreaking news that his younger brother, Jeff, had died after a long battle with cancer. John wasn't able to return to New York for the funeral. Jeff was buried two days after he died and his father felt it would be better for John to stay on Maui rather than rush home.

John's recollections remain vivid to this day. "It has always pained me that I was not able to be there to help the family deal with Jeff's death, even though we had talked about the possibility before I left for Maui.

"I think a few people expressed their condolences, and then that was the end of it. I never heard another word from my parents or any of my friends at home, many of whom had attended Jeff's funeral. Ironically, at the end of that summer on Maui and on my way back to New York, I stopped off in San Francisco to attend my grandfather's funeral. My father picked me up at the airport. He never once mentioned my brother during the two days we were together. When I got back home, I came to a house filled with grief and anger, but no words.

"My father lost his faith in God and my mother lost her reason for living. She was never able to overcome the blow of losing one child only to have another, my sister, diagnosed with cancer shortly thereafter. Even after spending hours with our mother in family counseling sessions we never got to the root of her grief. It was too painful to touch."

We all make choices. There is no right or wrong choice. No judgment.

The choice to live—really live—and the reasons for it are unique to each of us. Many of us do it for our survivors, as Patty did for two children who, though young adults, depended on her.

Some do it for those we lost. Hilary admonished Brittany, Ryan, and me on day one after Jimmy died. "We cannot let Jimmy's death take us down! That would make him so unhappy, and we will not make Jimmy unhappy."

Others may stick around because they believe this is all there is or they're not so sure what may come next will be better than what we have here.

Contemplating a choice to live also forces us to ask ourselves the obvious question: *What will I do with my life? What will give my life meaning?*

Dr. Frankl contemplated this conundrum in *Man's Search for Meaning*: "We must never forget that we may also find meaning in life even when confronted with a hopeless situation, when facing a fate that cannot be changed. For what then matters is to bear witness to the uniquely human potential at its best, which is to transform a personal tragedy into triumph, to turn one's predicament into a human achievement. When we are no longer able to change a situation—just think of an incurable disease such as inoperable cancer—we are challenged to change ourselves."

The Leslies' situation seemed utterly hopeless. The clock could not be wound back on the terrorist attack that claimed the life of their only child. Life no longer held any meaning or purpose. Those died with Nicolas. However, with the passage of time and a lot of help from the "Gifts from Nick," the Leslies surrendered to the challenge to change themselves.

After moving to Hawaii, as they learned to live with their horrific loss, and how to wear it in public, they began to help others.

They established the Victory of the People scholarship fund at Cal Berkeley, which provides students like Nick with spending money so they can attend cultural events, travel, and interact with the locals and share ideas when they study abroad.

They volunteer with Access Surf, a local nonprofit that empowers people of all ages with disabilities to learn to swim and surf. Conrad says, "The smiles from the participants and the looks upon their parents' faces watching their child with special needs catch her first wave is pure love."

The Leslies are both very active with Helping Parents Heal, and have shared their story in numerous TV and newspaper interviews and talks with fellow grieving parents.

I have been privileged to watch their emergence from near total darkness into Shining Light Parents and ambassadors of Frankl's message that it is possible to *transform a personal tragedy into triumph.*

I've also witnessed this with many of my other Fraternity brothers-in-loss.

As mentioned earlier, Jeffrey and Anita Miller's daughter, Ariana, succumbed in 2008 after a long battle with congenital heart disease. The talented 13-year-old loved music and visits from her music therapist while she was hospitalized. Ariana created two albums of songs she wrote and recorded during her therapy sessions. The Millers honored her memory by establishing the Ariana Miller Music with Heart Program. Together with the nonprofit Resounding Joy, they have raised hundreds of thousands of dollars to provide free music therapy for thousands of children with heart disease and other life-threatening afflictions in San Diego, mostly through benefit concerts featuring young San Diego talent.

On August 9, 2010, two years to the day after Jimmy died, Amanda Post, 18, was killed along with three others in a fiery crash while driving back to San Diego from a high-altitude Olympic training camp at Mammoth Mountain. In June she had graduated with honors shortly after winning CIF-San Diego gold medals in both the girls' 800 meters and as the anchor for the girls' 4 x 400-meter relay, and competing in the 800-meter state championships in Fresno. She had planned to head for Cal Poly San Luis Obispo the following month on a track scholarship.

The loss of their beloved daughter was devastating to her parents, but they understood they had a choice to make. As Missy recalled, "We realized we could either let this destroy us or we could live to honor her." Greg said, "We wanted her to be remembered not for how she died, but for how she lived. She absolutely radiated her joy for life."

So Greg and Missy created the Amanda Post Foundation to award scholarships to outstanding female student-athletes graduating from San Diego County high schools with a superior GPA, who will be entering a four-year university and running competitively for their NCAA track or cross-country teams. Over the past nine years, Amanda's foundation has provided 60 four-year scholarships and one-year grants to help these amazing women reach for their dreams.

The Millers' other daughter, Delaney, received one of Amanda's scholarships, and that's how they met the Posts and Jeffrey joined our Fraternity.

John and Alison Barry's 22-year-old son died tragically in 2012. Ian "Poods" Barry was a passionate skateboarder and surfer, beloved by everyone he met. Together with their daughter, Kiva, the Barrys launched Rollin' From the Heart in honor and memory of Poods. The foundation serves at-risk and underserved youth throughout San Diego County, teaching them to skateboard, surf, and camp.

There are many ways we who have lost someone we deeply love can help others. First and foremost, choosing to live helps your family. Your choice emboldens them to choose the same. It also spares them the crushing wave of another loss, be it an early death, or of someone just giving up on life and withdrawing into a personal cell.

Your choice to live helps your friends and colleagues. They are observing you, and you may not realize that you are a teaching moment for them. Most have not experienced unbearable loss. What you do and how you reconstruct your mind and life will be imprinted in their memory banks and revisited when they—or another friend, family member, or colleague—are hit by a crippling loss.

My mentor, Brian, chose to live, as we explored in "I Know You Think This Will Never Get Better." Sometimes, because of our own experience with devastating loss, we are presented with opportunities to help others with this choice.

When people you know—or don't—have suffered a crushing loss, and you reach out and talk to them about yours, you are helping them immensely. Seeing you standing there, out in the world, doing whatever it is you're doing, coupled with the fact that you are actually able to talk to them about the "unthinkable," gives them hope and makes them feel less of a victim and less alone with their loss.

You don't have to give talks, do TV interviews, start foundations and scholarship funds, write books, or run grief groups to help others. You don't have to do what Richard Page does and cold-call fathers who have lost kids. Some of the fathers in our Fraternity are particularly helpful with the new dads just by sharing their stories of how their children died. Then they listen compassionately as the new dad tells his story, most often for the first time in front of a group.

Chris Ramirez often shares his story, "I'm Christian," with the new dads, who have tears rolling down their cheeks when Chris gets to the part where his father holds his eyes closed for five seconds. Grandpa's last message gives them hope. *Yes, my grandson Christian came to visit me this morning and is waiting for me on the other side.*

By sharing his story, Chris opens the door and emboldens others to share experiences with their departed children that can't be explained; stories the dads are not comfortable sharing with others who can't comprehend their pain.

Each of us finds those avenues and opportunities for helping others that feel right and manageable. As I said, if all you can do is choose life, be there for your family, show up with your friends and colleagues, and be a compassionate listener, you are helping others.

Then there are those like the Leslies who take helping others to places that are well outside most of our comfort zones. Conrad finds most rewarding the talks he gives to inner-city high school students about suicide. Failing a class, a breakup, or being bullied may feel like the end of the world to them. He is compelled to share the nightmare of losing his only child in a terrorist attack because "it is heartbreaking to realize how many students take their own lives because of problems that pale by comparison. My goal is to help these kids realize if Paola and I could survive the darkest night of our souls, they too can overcome their problems.

"My message to these students is that you don't always have a choice on what can happen to you in life, but you do have a choice as to how you react. Never give up. Surrendering to something that can't be changed or is out of your control is not a bad thing. Surrendering is not the same as giving up. It's the realization that if you can't do anything to change something, you must now change course and try something different."

He likes to use the analogy of those in battle. "Some heroes are often defined not by how they handled victory—it's easy to handle victory—but how they handled defeat."

Dr. Frankl, Patty Reis, Kerry Cline, Hugh Sill, Susan Hannifin-MacNab, Richard Page, Chris Ramirez, the Leslies, Posts, Millers, and Barrys are some of my heroes.

They are beautiful people.

May you always do for others and let others do for you.
—Bob Dylan, *Forever Young*

BONUS STORIES: MAYBE LAST, BUT NOT LEAST

PLEASE DO NOT be misled by the placement of these stories. They are some of my favorites, each of them stands strong on its own, and we just had to include them.

Jeff Phair, in his beautiful story "I Love You, Dad," explores more deeply the complex father-son relationship and how, once again, it can be mended by letters; in Jeff's case, by the ones he wrote to his dad.

Linda Kwasny was the first person Hilary reached out to for help in those first, intensely dark weeks after Jimmy died. In the deeply moving story, "From the Heart," Linda shares how she and her family made the choice to live following the death of her 16-year-old daughter by suicide in 1991.

And just when we think Rabbi Regina Sandler-Phillips's work with us is done, she pops back up in the super-synchronistic story "Sent by a Rabbi," as further validation of one of my favorite quotes from the TV series *Touch*: *If two points are destined to touch, the Universe will always find a way to make the connection.*

My Fraternity-in-Loss brother, Bill Canepa, shares an incredible story of how his youngest son, Sean, enlisted the help of a feathered friend to send his family a mind-blowing message of peace and comfort on his first Angel Date. "Hope Is a Thing with Feathers" and "Sent by a Rabbi" are also beautiful testaments to the strong gravitational force that brings grieving parents together. And that our children's fingerprints are all over it.

And, of course, I have to share another Jimmy story, "Now's the Time," of the help and guidance he continues to send us, this time with the daunting task we parents must eventually confront—cleaning out their bedrooms.

I LOVE YOU, DAD

by Jeff Phair

MY DAD DIED in 2010 at the age of 88. David Phair was born on December 7, 1921. He moved to San Diego as a young boy and attended Hoover High School and San Diego State College. The Japanese attacked Pearl Harbor on his 20th birthday, and he promptly enlisted in the Navy and completed officers' training school, then fought in the Pacific Theater.

When I was a boy, I tried to get Dad to tell me about the war—a young boy's morbid curiosity—but he never would. He was a very stoic and unemotional person. After years of pestering him, he finally gave in and said, "Jeff, I will talk about the war this one time, but never ask me again."

He told me that he piloted small landing craft ferrying soldiers from the huge troop ships to the shores of the Japanese occupied islands being attacked. He'd drop off 100 men on the beach and by the time he came back with another load of soldiers, the bodies of half the men he had dropped off 15 minutes earlier were floating out to sea.

Dad showed no emotion in his very short description of what

he did in the war, and he never spoke of it again. He dealt with the atrocities of war by suppressing them. In society today, we now understand what PTSD is. It permanently scarred my dad all those years ago.

I now realize the same emotional detachment was also true of my friends who came back from Vietnam, the lucky ones who did come back.

I grew up as the only son, with three sisters. Dad was always warm and demonstrative in his affection for his daughters, but not with me. He was very hard on me. I got good grades, but he was disappointed that I wasn't class valedictorian. I'd run for 200 yards and score four touchdowns in a game and he would ask me why I didn't score five. I grew up wondering if Dad loved me, because he never said it to me. Whatever my accomplishments were didn't seem to be good enough.

My dad made me work every summer as a teenager. I worked as a laborer building small rental homes on my family's ranch in Bonita near San Diego. I dug the footings and foundations by hand because it was cheaper to pay me $1.15 an hour than rent a gas-powered Ditch Witch. I mixed concrete in a wheelbarrow and poured small sections of the footings at a time because it was cheaper than bringing in a concrete truck with a boom pump. I realize now that Dad wasn't just being frugal. He was teaching me the value of hard work, and that going to college was a much better alternative.

I spent my sophomore year in college studying in Mexico City. When I came back, I had a beard and shoulder-length hair. Dad looked at me and said that I had probably spent the year in Mexico as a drug dealer. He kicked me out of the house and cut me off financially.

Dad had built a successful chain of men's clothing stores in San Diego. He was a three-piece-suit, button-down-collar, and wingtip man. He was embarrassed that I looked like a "hippie" and wasn't his clone.

I converted my grandmother's garage into a studio apartment. I spent the next seven years working in the restaurant business as a bus boy, waiter, and cook to put myself through college, an MBA program, and law school. Maybe it was Dad's plan to toughen me up through facing adversity. But I don't know, because we rarely talked for ten years.

When I married my wonderful wife, Julie, 40 years ago, she told me that I had to be the first one to reach out to Dad to reestablish a relationship. She told me to write Dad a letter and talk about fun things we did together when I was a boy. Most importantly, Julie told me that I had to sign the letter "Love, Jeff." Dad never acknowledged my first letter, but Julie encouraged me to keep writing.

Several times a year, I would write to him and reminisce about a camping trip we went on with Indian Guides when I was seven or eight years old. Or I would share stories about fun things I was doing with Julie and our three sons. For over 30 years, I wrote him what Julie referred to as "Dad/Son love letters." He never acknowledged any of them. When I would see him, I always ended our visit by saying, "I love you, Dad." He never said that to me in return. I now realize that it wasn't me—his generation of men didn't say "I love you" to another man, not even their sons.

As our three sons were growing up, I would write them several times a year, recounting fun things we had done as a family. But the real purpose of my letters was to tell my sons that I loved them. I did not want my sons to grow up, as I did, wondering if their dad loved them.

When the boys were too young to read, Julie would take them to the mailbox to pick up my letters to each of them. What a thrill to get a letter addressed to them! Julie would read each letter aloud to them, then put the letters in a small wooden Memory Box on top of the desk in each boy's bedroom. I wrote my "love letters" to my sons for over 25 years.

All of my sons, now in their 30s, lived at home until they got married. When each son got married, Julie gave his Memory Box to his wife so she could know more about her husband growing up. More importantly, my letters to my sons, shared with their wives, reinforced the importance of telling their children that they love them.

Love should be expressed with heartfelt words, not by giving a child a new bike for Christmas or a video game on their birthday. All three of my sons live in San Diego within 20 minutes of Julie and me in Bonita. We have Sunday dinners together almost every week. They never leave our home without my telling them I love them, and them saying, "I love you, Dad."

I was visiting my dad the day he had a massive heart attack and stroke at age 88. In the emergency room, the doctors told me there was nothing they could do. He had only a few hours to live. I sat by his bed holding his hand. He was still conscious but could not talk. I remembered all the letters I had written him over the years. I started re-telling him some of the fun things we had done together: a trip to Disneyland; having our tent collapse at night while camping in the mountains; hiking together in Yosemite, one of God's greatest creations.

For two hours I talked and he listened with a smile. Just before he passed, I held him in my arms and hugged him. I told him that I loved him. I had waited 59 years to hear him say the same to me. But he was unable to do so because of the stroke. He smiled and nodded, and a few minutes later he was gone.

Several months later, I cleaned out his office, the same office he had gone to for 60 years. He had saved and neatly organized everything that had ever come into his office: thousands of postmarked stamps and old rubber bands, 60-year-old newspaper sale ads from his clothing stores.

One drawer in his desk was locked. I could not find a key, so I pried it open. To my surprise there was an old cigar box, my dad's own Memory Box. Inside was every letter, over 100, that I had sent to him over the previous 30 years, stacked neatly in chronological order. On each letter he had written a short note: "Yes, I remember that camping trip"; "Yosemite was beautiful"; "Our trip to Disneyland was fun"; "Your sons are handsome like their Grandpa (HA HA)."

The very last letter I sent to Dad was just a few weeks before he passed away. At the bottom of the letter right below where I had written, "I love you, Dad," he had written "I love you too, son."

I broke down and cried like a baby.

FROM THE HEART

*The best way to find yourself is to lose
yourself in the service of others.*

—Mahatma Gandhi

LINDA AND RICH Kwasny's daughter, Andie, died by suicide in
1991. She was sixteen years old and a sophomore at Torrey Pines
High School. Andie had struggled with depression. The Kwasnys
created the Andie Kwasny Memorial Fund to support suicide prevention programs for youth. Linda became involved with Survivors
of Suicide and led a group of survivors in San Diego for over ten
years. She found this work healing. "Facing the fire—looking into
the eyes of others who have suffered the death of a loved one by
suicide—made me feel less alone with Andie's."

Rich and Linda had long held a dream of moving to Fiji. A
few years after Andie died, they sold everything and began years of
many trips back and forth to Fiji to plan and build a high-end Eco
Lodge on Beqa Island off the main island of Viti Levu. The Five-Star
Lalati Resort and Spa opened in 2000 and soon became a popular

destination for weddings. During construction there were rumors of locals seeing a pretty, young white woman with long brown hair walking on the beach or in the groves of palm trees.

In 2001, Linda was at the Lalati talking with a guest. She and her husband were the only guests at the resort. The woman asked Linda, "Who was that young white girl standing by the palm tree over by the pool a little earlier? Does she work here? Will she be joining us for lunch?" At Linda's urging, she described her in more detail. Linda went to her office and came back with a photo of Andie. "Is this the girl you saw?"

"Yes."

Linda was deeply unsettled as she explained to the unsuspecting guest what should have been the impossibility of her seeing Andie.

While Lalati was popular and doing well, there was something missing. Linda recalled, "We had over 100 joyful weddings, wonderful gatherings of families and guests, and yet the resort held no purpose for us." She and Rich thought they would be helping the villagers on this very remote island by bringing good jobs and other opportunities. "The guests were 'interesting' to them. There wasn't a huge motivation to earn and save money. They were happy and didn't need to be 'rescued.' At the end of the day, they taught us so much about priorities and living life in the moment."

But there was a disheartening absence of medical care on the island.

Linda had read about International Relief Teams, a nonprofit based in San Diego, providing medical and dental care in the South Pacific. She reached out to one of them, explaining, "We have this resort, there is no health care on our island..." Dr. Lance Hendricks visited Lalati on behalf of IRT. He is an anesthesiologist at Scripps Hospital in La Jolla and had been volunteering his services in Fiji for a number of years. Soon after their meeting, Lalati began to host relief teams who performed cataract surgeries for residents of Beqa and neighboring islands. They set up a clinic in the laundry area at the resort and also began providing basic dental care.

Within a year, Rich and Linda sold Lalati, moved back to Del Mar, and Lance and Linda started the Loloma Foundation. Over the past 19 years, Loloma—which in Fijian means "from the heart"—has shipped over $32 million worth of medication, medical and dental supplies, and equipment to Fiji and the Solomon Islands; organized over 60 missions to 150 villages; and treated over 100,000 patients by volunteer physicians, surgeons, and dentists. Annually, for two months, volunteer surgeons from the U.S. travel to a remote hospital on Taveuni Island to perform specialized surgeries, free of charge, for the people of Fiji.

Linda remains very active with the nonprofit foundation as a director and the project coordinator for the missions. She said, "The Loloma Foundation reshaped and repurposed our lives. Rich and I are happy, and I can even say joyful and grateful."

She talked about choice. "We consider ourselves lucky. We all have a choice to make and we chose to live after Andie's suicide. It wasn't easy, but we had to be there for Andie's younger brother and for each other. We stumbled upon the opportunity to give back, and to turn our family's tragedy of losing a daughter much too early into something that helps so many extend and improve the quality of their lives."

Linda reflected, "I think of it as 'paying the rent.' We're provided a place and time to live, learn, and grow on this planet, and giving back is our way of compensating the creator."

I asked Linda how she feels now about those who saw Andie at Lalati all those years ago.

"I think Andie wanted to let Rich, her brother, and me know she is OK, and we were doing the right thing by going to Fiji."

⋘

Loloma Foundation's work on the Solomon Islands caught my eye. I mentioned to Linda that my father spent all of 1944 on Bougainville fighting the Japanese during World War II. Linda knew of this very remote island in the Solomons and had heard stories from some of the elders who survived the Japanese occupation and liberation by the Americans. She said, "The natives were terrified of the Japanese soldiers. They inflicted horrific, unspeakable atrocities upon them. If your father spent a year living and fighting on that island, there is no way he came home the same man as when he left."

SENT BY A RABBI

I RECEIVED AN email in November of 2019 from a man named John with the subject: *Sent by Rabbi Regina.*

I opened the email with abundant curiosity and anticipation. It read, *We have never met, but I have a quick story to tell you. This past weekend we were in Brooklyn's Prospect Park for a tree planting and bench dedication for my daughter Erica, who passed away suddenly in an accident in Brooklyn on August 30, 2011.*

John and his wife, who now live in San Diego, Erica's three sisters, and a collection of close friends gathered in the park and planted a serviceberry tree. They also decorated a protective fence surrounding the tree and placed a picture of Erica on the fence with the message *Your presence will always be cherished as a lasting memory to everyone you touched.*

John went on to tell me that the following day, he and his wife and their good friend Karen strolled back to the park to sit on Erica's bench, and just enjoy the cool sunny day.

As we approached Erica's tree, we noticed a woman reading the sign on the protective fence and looking at her picture. As we got closer, I said hello, but she had already turned and was walking away. Karen was bolder and called out, "What do you think of the tree?"

The woman stopped, turned, and said that she frequently walks in the park but had not noticed this tree before. The sign was moving to her, and the picture of Erica was very nice.

John's group introduced themselves and explained what they'd been up to the past couple of days. The woman said, "I'm Regina Sandler-Phillips," and she let them do most of the talking, about Erica and her life and death, and also about the magic that Erica brings when their family is around the place of her passing.

John explained, "Our daughter Erica was riding her bike home from work a few blocks from this park. She struck some construction debris, fell, and was struck and killed by an automobile. That was eight years ago. She was 29."

After they talked some more, Regina mentioned she was a rabbi and suggested, "You should look up a blog, 'Write Me Something Beautiful,' hosted by a man named Casey Gauntt who also lives in San Diego."

John read several of our stories on the website on the plane ride back to San Diego and decided to reach out to me. *I find in your stories the patterns that I have experienced dealing with friends and family and the expression of grief that never leaves us, even after eight years. We, too, cherish the signs Erica sends along to let us know she is still here with us.*

He wrote of the serendipity of the meeting in the park. *I know in most people's minds, meeting Rabbi Regina in that park was a totally random coincidence. But you and I both know that experiences happen that are meant to be...the signposts they leave for us...to assure us they are still here.*

It's well within the realm of probability John and his family would run into Rabbi Regina in that park. She frequently walks there, and they had made a recent improvement that caught the rabbi's eye.

But there are almost eight and a half million people in New York City. And they just happened to meet up with one of a handful I know, one year after the rabbi reached out to console me for our loss of Jimmy ten years earlier, who had also been struck and killed by an automobile.

Jimmy's fingerprints were all over this. So were Erica's.

And yet, this wasn't our first rodeo. We have been blessed with many wonderful synchronicities and NLEs. We continue to experience that same jolt of energy, electricity, when they land. But we are less and less surprised when they do. As Father Pat observed, we've come to expect these God moments.

I did some searching. Erica had been living in New York pursuing her lifelong passion as a professional modern dancer. She was a devoted student of Buddhism and active with social causes in the community.

I got back to John the following day. I shared with him our own "random" connection with Rabbi Regina a year earlier and that it was the rabbi who put the spotlight on the fact that we on this earthly plain can help with the healing of our loved ones on the other side, just as they help us here with ours.

Jimmy and Erica, who had never met here, as far as I know, shared so much in common.

Taken too soon, tragically, suddenly, and violently, in their 20s in the month of August.

Deeply passionate about the arts, dancing, writing, and certainly much more.

Buddhists at their core.

They both have benches in parks.

We didn't plant a tree, but we adopted a big tree across from Jimmy's bench that everyone calls Jimmy's Tree.

And I closed with, "Yes, many people probably think we're crazy."

"Sent by a Rabbi" is dedicated in loving memory of Erica Louise, who continues to dance with the stars and heavens. Please visit Rabbi Regina's website, WaysofPeace.org, to learn more about the wonderful work they do.

HOPE IS THE THING WITH FEATHERS: WELCOME HOME, SEAN

by Bill Canepa

"Hope" is the thing with feathers -
That perches in the soul -
And sings the tune without the words -
And never stops - at all -

And sweetest - in the Gale - is heard -
And sore must be the storm -
That could abash the little Bird
That kept so many warm -

I've heard it in the chillest land -
And on the strangest Sea -
Yet - never - in Extremity,
It asked a crumb - of me.

—Emily Dickinson (1830–1886)

OUR 18-YEAR-OLD SON, Sean, died of an accidental overdose on March 30, 2008. We had become acquainted with Hilary and Casey Gauntt after the passing of their son, Jimmy, in August of that year. Even though we live within two blocks of each other, we may never have met except for our shared tragedies. The two boys went to the same high school, but Jimmy was five years older.

Sharing that unfortunate bond, my wife Cathie and Hilary soon became friends and soul mates. They were able to laugh and cry together, as only they could understand what each was going through.

A few months after they had met, Hilary told Cathie about Tarra, a psychic and medium from Sedona her family had met just before Christmas. I have always been a skeptical person by nature, but when you lose a child the finality of that loss is overwhelming. You want to believe that, somehow, they are not completely gone.

We knew that his spirit would be haunted if his death was responsible for the disintegration of our family. With uncertain hope, we agreed to do a reading with Tarra in San Diego. Kevin and Kyle, Sean's older brothers, also showed up.

During the reading, Tarra described our backyard with uncanny accuracy and said that a bird would fly up to our windows and spread its wings as a sign from Sean. We took note of her prediction, but we have lots of birds in our yard. How would we ever know that one of them was a messenger from our son?

Several months later, the first anniversary of Sean's passing was upon us. We dreaded that milestone for weeks in advance. Kevin and Kyle came home so we could all be together. At about 9:00 a.m. on Sean's Angel Date, while I was brushing my teeth, Cathie called out that a big white bird had flown up to our back door and landed on the arm of a nearby chair.

When I rushed to the door, I also saw what I thought was a dove perched on that chair. I went outside and crept closer and closer.

Cathie whispered, "Don't frighten it," but I kept approaching and sat down in an adjacent chair a few feet away.

It was then that I saw a homing tag attached to the bird's ankle. It wasn't a dove, but a beautiful snow-white pigeon. And that bird stayed in that same position until late that afternoon.

Almost eight hours.

Kevin took a close-up photo of the pigeon, which is prominently displayed in our home together with photos of Sean.

We had bought tickets for all of us to see a movie starring Will Ferrell at 5:30 in Del Mar. Perhaps a little humor might take some weight off our hearts. Yet we questioned how we could leave with the bird still there. After all, wasn't it our link to Sean? On cue, the bird spread its wings and flew off.

The homing pigeon had fulfilled its purpose. It provided our family with comfort and reassurance in our time of grief.

We have never forgotten that day. Cathie immediately developed a love and passion for bird-watching and photography.

We believe that Sean, or an angel or God in the heavens, sent us that beautiful bird, on that particular day and time, with a message for us that Sean is okay and at peace. The peace it provided to our family that day and for many days and years to come has been immeasurable.

We dedicate this in loving memory of Sean Alexander Canepa.

NOW'S THE TIME

A COUPLE OF years ago we began a much-anticipated project to completely remodel the downstairs room in our house that Hilary and I had been using as our home offices over the previous ten years. Very exciting, right? Yes, but with one big catch—this was Jimmy's room, and it is filled with Jimmy.

This isn't the first time we've faced this daunting task. As I wrote in the chapter "The Rolex" in *Suffering Is the Only Honest Work*, Jimmy was renting a bohemian-style cabin in Laurel Canyon and pursuing his career in writing and acting in Los Angeles. A month after he died, Brittany and I drove to L.A. and met Jimmy's close friends John Dale and Evan Nicholas to clean out Jimmy's place. Although it was very hard and emotional, there were actually a lot of light moments and laughter triggered mostly by Jimmy's eclectic taste—or lack thereof—in clothes, his very hip selection of mostly jazz LPs, and his enormous collection of books, half in Spanish.

We boxed up the books, and I brought them home and put them up in our attic. John and Evan donated the clothes and what little furniture there was to a Hollywood community resource center, and each of us selected at least one thing of Jimmy's to keep. Brittany had already placed dibs on his writing table, which used to be her desk and that I had refinished for Jimmy. Evan selected the old espresso machine. John took the turntable and a few albums. I grabbed his well-worn leather jacket, with a threadbare Nordstrom's label, that he bought at Goodwill. I wear that jacket every chance I get.

Back home I took some time going through his things in his bedroom, like the backpack he brought home that last night and the drawers of his two nightstands.

My feeble efforts mostly involved packing more books and his extensive baseball card collection into boxes and hauling those up to the attic. The rest of his things were left in the three closets, nightstands, and the built-in cabinets. And that's where they resided for almost ten years.

We're talking about a lot of stuff: all of his original poems, stories, and screenplays, his jazz saxophone music, two saxophones and a flute, hundreds of photos, report cards and newspaper clippings. I'm pretty sure every card he ever wrote to us was in one of the drawers. There was his baseball glove and three footballs autographed by several Chargers players. The closets were home to the outfits he wore to proms and to Ryan and Brittany's wedding, the cowboy boots, leather chaps, and vest he wore every day from ages two to four, and a never-worn Torrey Pines High School letterman's jacket. "No better way to start a fight with kids from rival schools," he'd explained when I asked why he didn't wear it.

A box of trophies from youth soccer, Little League, and Pop Warner, and hundreds of CDs of his favorite music, some purchased but mostly his own playlists of burned favorites, needed to be dealt with before the remodel. There was a ton more of his books, four shopping bags of condolence cards, and the six guest books signed at his memorial service. And, of course, his king-sized bed.

Everything had to be taken out of his room before the demolition began. I offered to do the heavy lifting and make a first pass. Hilary gave me license to decide what to keep and toss. I promised myself I would set aside those things I felt needed a thumbs-up or down from Hilary or Brittany.

Fortunately, I had recently retired and had quite a bit of free time. I dedicated the next two weeks to spending some quiet, quality time with my son. It was very much like uncovering an ancient city long hidden under the accumulation of centuries, layers of discoveries in each drawer, file cabinet, folder, and closet that held all of these memories and markers from each of his 24 years with us. I took my time. He and we had accumulated so much because he accomplished so much.

Some decisions were easy, like the floppy discs for the Nintendo games—into the trash bag. We would keep all of his writings, including the eight drafts of the last screenplay he was working on, *Now's the Time.* Like F. Scott Fitzgerald, Faulkner, and Van Gogh, I continue to believe Jimmy will be posthumously famous one day. I'm reminded of the lines from The Band Perry's hauntingly beautiful song "If I Die Young":

A penny for your thoughts? Oh no,
I'll sell them for a dollar
They're worth so much more
After I'm a goner.

Maybe then you'll hear
The words I've been singing
Funny when you're dead how
People start listening.

Our medium Tarra had instructed us years ago to keep his musical instruments for the yet-to-be-born grandkids. The two saxophones and the flute stayed, but I tossed the box of saxophone music and two of the footballs signed by the Judases, aka the ex-San Diego Chargers. I kept the one signed by Junior Seau. He was a friend of Jimmy's and mine.

The clothes not attacked by moths were donated to the Encinitas

Community Resource Center—which by the way was really excited about the letterman's jacket.

I created three "I'm not sure" piles for Hilary, Brittany, and Ryan to peruse. Ryan chose Jimmy's well-traveled leather briefcase, some books with Jimmy's chicken-scratch notes in the margins and, for his boys, Jimmy's first Little League home run ball. Hilary and Brittany kept all photos and everything he ever wrote to them. No one wanted the cowboy boots, vest, and chaps.

I couldn't part with the condolence cards and guest books, not yet anyway. Maybe someday I'll have the fortitude to go through them.

I continue to keep his cell phone and wallet, including the three $20 bills tucked inside, in a nice enameled cigar box–sized case.

I wouldn't go so far as to call it a purge, but at the end of the day we had made a sizeable dent. There remain hundreds of photos in bags and boxes that I will cull through and digitize. Another great retirement project. And ten-plus boxes of books, baseball cards, and Jimmy's writings safe in the attic. Maybe in another ten years we'll be ready to take another look at them.

It felt really good to spend so much time with Jimmy through all of the things he touched, wore, and wrote, and all that which was written about him. I kept it together pretty well, with one major exception. And that was when I got the message from Jimmy's good pals, John and Evan, that they were going to run the Los Angeles Marathon. Jimmy had run that marathon, his one and only, in 2007. The boys had set up a GoFundMe account to raise money for The Jimmy Gauntt Memorial Award given out annually since 2010 by the USC English Department to top graduating seniors. I completely broke down and cried harder than I'd cried in a long time. When I finished, I felt cleansed. Evan and John raised over $7,000 for The Jimmy.

That left his bed. I felt it important for Hilary to make that decision.

On Good Friday, a wonderful nonprofit organization, Just in

Time, that benefits young men and women transitioning out of foster care to independent living picked up Jimmy's bed, the lamps, and his nightstands. All three young men who came to the house to pick them up were raised in foster homes. Tearfully we watched as their rental truck drove away. We know they will find another good home for Jimmy's bed.

It was time.

It was time for us to let some of Jimmy's things go. After ten years, we knew that stuff isn't what keeps us connected to him. Those are fingerprints, but that isn't Jimmy. All of my brothers- and sisters-in-loss confront this. Some are not ready to touch their child's bedroom for fear it will be interpreted as they are moving on and no longer remember or want to remember their child. Many of us fear that "the things" are all we have left.

Jimmy, in his gentle, persuasive way, let us know, "It's okay. Now's the time."

The End

APPENDIX

GOD MOMENTS: SOME TOOLS FOR RECEIVING MORE

SYNCHRONICITIES, VISITATIONS, SIGNS, and messages from those on the other side, or as Father O'Malley likes to call them, "God moments," are all around us. And as Father Pat pointed out, the tragedies of lost loved ones have moved us to a different plane with different understandings and enhanced our access to the God moments.

My dad and Jimmy, Nicolas Leslie, Sean Canepa, Christian Ramirez, David Cline, Erica, and Ben are not in a special category of souls. I have not met a single person who has lost someone they love who has not experienced a God moment. However, many express dismay at not receiving more.

Here are a few suggestions for receiving more God moments.

Acknowledge, write, talk about, and otherwise share your God moments with family and friends and even those you just meet who might benefit. These aren't just for you. They are for the collective "US" and meant to be shared.

Ask for more. Be specific about what you want and why. Visiting us in our dreams is one of the easier things for our loved ones to accomplish. Invite them to do so. When they do come in, write the dreams down in a journal. Acknowledging and preserving these visits helps keep the portal open for more.

Look for and act upon opportunities to **deeply connect with others** who have suffered loss. Your loss has put you on a different plane. You are uniquely experienced and qualified to help others. Those who have not suffered unbearable loss, no matter how many degrees they may have earned, simply cannot connect at the depth and level of understanding and compassion as those who have.

Your grief is more than a heavy load you carry. That bag of rocks is also filled with tools to help your fellow sufferers. The more you connect with and help others here, the more deeply and often you connect with loved ones on the other side.

Work on mending relationships with your loved ones that may be broken or not as strong as you wish them to be. They may be hesitant to come through to you. It took my dad (and me) 38 years. Forgiveness is a powerful veil buster. When you are ready, forgive or ask for forgiveness. Remember, grief and the healing process is a two-way street. Our loved ones help us from their side, and we can help them from our side.

Put away any fear. It takes some grit to take those first steps into the rabbit hole. I'm reminded of an Eckhart Tolle mantra: *I will be fearless in my life.* I often say to myself, "What in the world do I have to be afraid of? The worst thing imaginable already happened to me." If you show no fear, this will embolden your loved ones to come through.

Don't be selfish with your grief and healing. One of my brothers-in-loss was scolded by his wife when he was in a "Why me, God?" funk over the death of his son. She reminded him, "Hey, I lost him, too!" Be mindful of and proactive with the suffering and needs of your spouse, your other kids, your greater family, and your loved one's friends. They lost him/her too, and they suffer mightily.

Unlock the doors. As a bereaved parent or sibling, you hold the keys to doors that only you can open and let others pass through to help with their healing. They want and need to talk to you and feel connected to the one they lost, too. Once again, the more you help others with their pain and healing, the more God moments will be revealed to further assist you with this good work.

Think big. As Rabbi Regina observed: *Death can yield into a healing of relationships through generations.* You are not limited to one, two, or even three generations. The "Hint" I received on Ancestry.com about the shipwreck that compelled me to write the story about Mary Sawyers Cook—four generations removed—was a God moment.

Be patient. There's no timetable for messages and signs to manifest and, besides, our concept of *time* isn't particularly relevant or applicable to the other side.

I suppose this all can be summed up with one word: connection. It's about staying connected with those who have left their physical bodies and those who remain here, repairing relationships, and removing other obstacles to connection with loved ones. It's about connecting deeply with others—family, friends, and those we just meet—and being open to receive messages, signs, and God moments from wherever they may originate, even if it's too hard to get our heads around them.

Our loved ones with whom we are forever entangled may seem impossibly far away and out of reach.

They are not.

No, we can't bring them "back" into their bodies. That particular "cure" is not available.

And yet, our loved ones remain forever connected to us, accessible to us, and always ready to share a God moment with us.

Do your work, and they will come.

CODY: PERMISSION TO GRIEVE

FOR OVER FOUR weeks in the summer of 2020, we had painters and hardwood floor guys crawling throughout our house. I'm blaming this on COVID-19. You know, all those things you let slide when you're zipping in and out of the house, spending more time outside than in. And then, after days, weeks, and months confined in various stages of lockdown, you begin to notice things. Things that pre-pandemic were only slightly irritating now just scream at you: *The carpet is trashed; I'm sick of the color of the ceiling in the family room; why did we ever carpet the staircases?*

Cody was one of the craftsmen installing meticulously cut and stained oak panels in our staircases. He's a talented and engaging young man, late 30s, long blond hair worn in a ponytail. Tattoos adorn his hands, chest, and back of his wiry frame, each one begging for a story to be revealed. He's a family man with three kids ages five to ten. I detected a Southern accent, maybe west Texas.

The second day on the job, Hilary and I were visiting with Cody. Light chat. He was in awe of our massive Torrey pine tree. He told us a little bit about his family. Cody and I went back into the house and, as he got back to work, he sprang the inevitable question.

"So, how many kids do you have?"

I did not skip a beat. "We have two. Our oldest, Brittany, is 40, and she and her husband and their two boys live close by in Santa Luz. Our son, Jimmy, was accidently struck and killed by a car walking home from a friend's house in 2008."

A bit of air was sucked out of the room. Cody paused his work and turned his pain-filled face to me. "I'm so sorry."

"Thank you," and I would have left it at that were it not for Cody's next questions.

"How old was your son?"

"Twenty-four."

Longer pause.

"How did you ever survive that?"

Decision time. Go with the conversation stopper? *It was really hard, but some way, somehow, we've gotten through it. Thanks for asking.*

Instead, I chose to tell Cody the abbreviated story about my father and how he came through to me years later with his letter.

When I got to my dad's last words in his letter… *I'll be around, anytime you want me…* and that it arrived on Jimmy's 25th birthday, Cody began to cry.

I explained that Jimmy was just starting his career as a professional writer and how he's been feeding me stories, which led to a website, and then a couple of books.

Cody then began to tell me about his parents' divorce several years earlier, and how hard it has been on him and his sister. "Dad's new, much younger, wife is very controlling. They travel a lot and my sister and I feel we're really not welcome. My sister also has three young kids and our dad has missed several of their birthdays. He just plain forgets. I'm not allowed to just drop by unannounced at their house—*my* house—the house I grew up in. I have to call first." He unloaded for a while.

Then, quickly flicking a tear away, Cody said, "I don't know why I'm telling you any of this. I never talk about it. And, heck, I still have my dad, and I can't even imagine what it would be like if I lost my sister. I'm sorry." Another tear flicked away.

I consoled Cody. "No need to apologize. One of the many things I've learned over the last years is we, particularly guys, are terrible at talking about our feelings, the tough stuff, anything that might show a chink in our armor. So let me ask you, how do you feel having shared your stuff with me?"

He said, "I feel better, a little lighter. I sure never thought I'd be crying on the job in front of a customer!"

We laughed and I said, "You see what happened here? I shared my truth—my bad stuff—with you. I didn't have to, and often I don't. But when I did, I opened the door for you. I gave you an opportunity to share something with me. We guys have a hard time doing this. But we need to. You and I just connected at a much deeper level by taking off some of our armor. It feels good, doesn't it?"

"It sure does."

Cody finished his work the next day. Before he left, I showed him my workshop in the garage where I make my birdhouses. I had him pick one out for his kids. I also gave him a copy of *Suffering*.

The next day, Cody swung by the house unannounced. He brought me a crate filled with several containers of customized wood stain and finishing lacquer, and a bunch of high-end sandpaper.

"I picked up some things from the shop that I thought you could use for your birdhouses. If you ever need anything, just let me know."

Before he took off, I asked him if I could take a photo of us. He said, "Sure. How about in front of the Torrey pine tree?" Perfect.

And it was. He and I both found solace in sharing, and we'll never be quite the same again.

MOURNING ALONE: CONDOLENCES IN THE TIME OF COVID-19

THE COVID-19 PANDEMIC is unlike anything the current generations have ever experienced. The worldwide loss of life, jobs, financial and emotional security, and hope is daunting. The numbers in the United States alone are mind-bending. As of January 2021, over 460,000 have died, millions remain out of work, and more than a quarter of the American population cannot afford to pay rent or buy enough food.

Even more chilling is the rise in signs of clinical depression and anxiety in adults and children. According to a study released in August of 2020 by the Centers for Disease Control and Prevention, 40% of U.S. adults are struggling with mental health and substance abuse issues. Though not surprising, the magnitude is deeply troubling.

This pandemic has left people to grieve in silence. Bodies pile up in crematories, funeral homes, and refrigerated trucks. The dead are reduced to a statistic on the nightly news and become fodder for the blame game. Funerals, if they can happen at all, are private. Survivors mourn the precious souls they've lost—alone.

The constraints imposed by the COVID-19 pandemic have obliterated our traditional means and rituals for grieving and paths to healing. Add to this the stress and anxiety from the huge upheavals in our economy and social and political environments and grief becomes overwhelming, and even small steps toward healing seem unattainable.

I also observed a sharp spike in the number of visits to the posts on our website for writing condolences when there's been a loss of a child or a death by suicide; over 10,000 per month. This was deeply concerning. I suspected this was not only directly tied to the rapidly rising number of people dying from COVID-19, but also to an accelerating loss of life as a result of the stress and anxiety caused by the pandemic and the reluctance or inability of many to obtain critical health care. I thought, "What can we do?"

Incorporating what we'd already learned, I wrote a new, more focused, post for our website: "How to Write Condolences to Someone You Don't Know Who Has Lost a Loved One to COVID-19." Then I began to write letters to strangers. I've encouraged friends, family, and followers of mine on Facebook, Instagram, LinkedIn, and Write Me Something Beautiful to do the same. Not surprisingly, I've received more than a little push-back and many questions:

> *This is way out of my comfort zone. What can*
> *I say about someone I don't even know to their*
> *friends and family who are also strangers?*
>
> *I don't know these people or how to get in touch with them.*
> *How do you find the loved ones and get a message to them?*
>
> *Won't people be offended or think it completely weird*
> *to receive a message from someone they don't know?*

Let's take these one by one.

What can you say about and to someone you don't know?

It is not as hard as you might think, especially if you come with a compassionate heart. As we shared in the "Condolences" chapter, there are six ingredients to writing a beautiful condolence letter. We've slightly modified these for letters to someone you don't know. You may not be able to incorporate all six, and that's okay. Do the best you can with what you've got. Remember, it is not so much about what you say. What is important is that you care enough to write anything at all.

Open strong with something from the heart. In her letter to Robert, Hilary opened with: *This message is for Robert, the loving son of the incredible Joan. I didn't know your mother, but the amazing story you wrote of her life brought me to tears and inspired me.*

You might also open with something like this: *This is for the family of Jane Doe. I am so deeply sorry for the loss of your beloved Jane to COVID-19. Although I did not know Jane, her loss and the lives of so many claimed by this ravaging disease has deeply saddened me, my family, and everyone in this country.*

Compliment the one who is gone or share a connection you may have. Hilary wrote that she and Robert's mother were the same age and were both mothers.

Try to find something online about the person and mention something you found interesting, that stood out, or that you have in common. In addition to obituaries, newspapers like the *Chicago Tribune, San Diego Union-Tribune, Los Angeles Times*, and *New York Times* have posted wonderful pieces where they have featured the victims of the disease with photos and short biographies.

If the loved one was in the service: *I know you will always be proud of John's service to his country.*

A shared love of something: *I read that Jimmy was an accomplished jazz saxophone player. I've played the sax all my life and Charlie Parker is one of my all-time favorites.*

A shared place: *I read that Jane lived in Roselle, Illinois. I grew* up in the town next door, Itasca, and went to Lake Park High School in Roselle.

A shared experience: *I too fought in Afghanistan after 9/11. I didn't serve with John, but I'm sure our boots covered much of the same ground and brought many of the same memories—some good, many not—home with us.*

Compliment the loved ones. *It takes courage to write an obituary and bare your soul and share with the masses the life and loss of your loved one. Thank you for telling us about your brother. I am fortunate to know a little more about him—the man, the friend, the co-worker, the son, the brother, the husband, the father.*

Say something uplifting. Hilary closed with, *I lost a son a decade ago and promise you this grief you must be feeling will soften, and the love you feel will always remain. God Bless your family.*

Sample Letters

This is the letter I wrote to the family of James Schwark, 68, who lived in Wheaton, Illinois. I posted it on Legacy.com. I found his bio in a special online tribute in the *Chicago Tribune* to those who have died in Illinois from COVID-19. I realized Jim and I had a lot in common.

FOR THE FAMILY OF JAMES SCHWARK

I am so deeply sorry for your loss. Although I didn't know Jim, I so enjoyed reading about him in the wonderful piece published by the Chicago Tribune on May 29 to honor and remember him and the too many others in Illinois who have been taken by this dreadful disease. "Wheaton" caught my eye. I grew up in nearby Itasca and went to Lake Park High School, graduating in 1968. And I, too, was an avid fan of the Cubbies. I still have the miniature bat I bought at Wrigley Field that Ernie Banks signed after a game in the early 1960s.

For us spread across the country, we watch the nightly news and see the daunting numbers of people who have passed from COVID-19. But we don't see their names or faces. We don't get to know who they really are. That is why I so appreciated the Tribune's effort. Jim is so much more than a statistic: He was a husband, dad, grandfather, friend, and colleague, deeply loved and missed by so many. I also loved reading about Jim's devotion to fitness, another thing we have in common.

I am profoundly sad for the loss of your Jim and the cumulative, crushing loss of so many others who have died from this disease. May you find some comfort in knowing the love you have for Jim and his love for you cannot be taken away, and that love will endure and always be there for and with you all. Please also know there are so many of us who feel your pain and deeply care about your healing and well-being. Blessings to you all.

Casey Gauntt

This is the opening to the letter I posted on Legacy.com for the family of Victor Pei, 65, who died of COVID-19 in May of 2020.

I am deeply sorry for your loss. Although I didn't know Victor, I so enjoyed reading about him in the Sunday, May 31 edition of the San Diego Union-Tribune. His ascension day, "May 7," caught my eye. That is the birthday of my wife of 47 years.

How do you find the loved ones and get a letter or message to them?

As I mentioned in "Condolences," most obituaries published in the newspapers make their way onto the Legacy.com platform. I read the obituary for Victor Pei in our San Diego paper. I searched "Victor Pei" and was taken right to Legacy.com.

To find COVID-19 victims in your area, you can also try searching COVID-19 + Legacy. com + Obituaries + Your City.

Won't people be offended or think it completely weird to receive a message from someone they don't know?

Robert's reply to Hilary's compassionate message speaks volumes on this question.

What Hilary did was pure and simple. She wrote a few heartfelt words and posted a message with nearly the same impact as if she had grabbed this young man and hugged him into her bosom.

It was powerful because it was genuine and from the depths of Hilary's soul. She knew what his mother's only child was feeling. The mother-son bond is strong and universal.

Hilary knew how alone we can feel with our grief. When we're suffering, we so welcome a heartfelt touch, message, some acknowledgment. Hilary felt Robert's considerable pain—his grief—through the precious words he wrote in the obituary for his mom.

Keep in mind, when survivors write obituaries for their loved ones, they are taking a big leap out of their comfort zones. They are revealing and sharing personal information and their feelings in a very public way. Most of us are just not comfortable doing this.

But think about it. Why do they write and publish their tributes to their loved one in the papers?

Because they want people to read them—and not just family, friends, and colleagues. They cry for people to read them and know a little something more about their precious ones.

Hilary's simple message of kindness and compassion let Robert know she heard him loud and clear, and that he was not alone with his loss.

We received several condolence letters from people who didn't know Jimmy or us. His death, our suffering, struck an emotional chord and they reached out. Some had lost children and, although they didn't "know" us, they knew only too well our pain and the long road ahead of us.

The fact that people made the compassionate, even brave, step to connect with us was deeply moving. They cared. We were not alone.

In the "Condolences" chapter and how-to-write-condolences posts on the website I've highlighted several "DON'TS."

Here's one more.

Don't expect a reply.

Although you might get one, like Hilary did from Robert, a reply to a condolence letter is never required and should not be expected. Especially from someone you don't know. You are sending words of comfort and compassion to ones who are suffering. It's about them, not you.

However, I have to admit, it is very gratifying to receive a message back. So far I'm batting over .500 with my letters to families of COVID-19 victims. Here is the message I received from Jim Schwark's son:

Casey, I just wanted to send a quick thank you for your kind words. Reading such genuine comments regarding someone you had not met was a wonderful pick-me-up this weekend. Stay well and go Cubs!

And I received this message from Victor's sister the day after I posted mine on Legacy:

Dear Mr. Gauntt,

I am moved by your heartfelt words of empathy in the passing of my dear brother Victor from COVID-19 in NYC on May 7, the date of your wife's birthday. Wow, how gracious that you, who did not even know Victor, sent these wonderful words of condolences.

Yes, every human being is of great value, and every loss brings unspeakable grief. I believe that humans are created in the image of God and deserve utmost respect and caring. We have more in common than we can fully appreciate. As we share joys and sorrows in life, we realize that relationships with our Creator and with each other are the most meaningful, giving us purpose for living.

And, yes, our love for Victor and his love for us will never be lost. Our faith in a gracious and loving God is giving us a peace that passes understanding. We mourn, but with a hope that allows us tears of deep sorrow mingled with tears of joy and thanksgiving.

Kind regards, and deep appreciation, with best wishes to you and Mrs. Gauntt,

Most sincerely,

Eva

ACKNOWLEDGMENTS

They say it takes a village to raise a child. Well, it took a village and then some to birth this book. There are so many to acknowledge and thank because so many contributed to this book from both sides of the veil and across many generations. In no particular order, I extend my deepest gratitude to:

My steady, brilliant, and courageous editor, Jan Weeks, who once again climbed into the rabbit hole with me to pull another book together and do her best to beat the lawyer out of me.

My old friends and muses-in-chief, George Blystone and Mike Lueth, for allowing me back into your lives, letting me bounce my crazy ideas off you, and always being so generous and frank with your sage insights and feedback.

Rabbi Regina Sandler-Phillips for your compassionate wisdom, showing us another dimension of helping our loved ones on the other side with their healing, and further evidence it's never too late to express condolences, particularly to people you don't know.

Chris Lynn, our Blue Jean Mystic, for sharing your incredible gifts and helping my father to finally come through with his messages of love, gratitude, and hope.

My good friend, filmmaker, and collaborator, Steve Date, for creating a beautiful homepage for the book and, well, for everything.

Emily Sue Buckberry, I will never be able to thank you enough for finding and safeguarding my father's letter and getting it to me when I needed it the most.

Jimmy's "big bro" John Dudek. Jimmy will always be your best man, and you will always be his.

Damon and Chrissy at Damonza for designing another awesome book cover.

My copy editor extraordinaire, Lisa Wolff.

Elizabeth Boisson and Irene Vouvalides, my sisters-in-loss, for all of the wonderful work you do with Helping Parents Heal and helping others suffer less.

Those who have shared their hard-earned wisdom with us: Elisabeth Kübler-Ross, Viktor Frankl, Emily Dickinson, Susan Hannifin-MacNab, Tom Zuba, Dr. Alan Wolfelt, Mark Nepo, Donna Nakazawa, Bonnie McEneaney, Father Patrick J. O'Malley, Monsignor Clement J. Connolly, David Lindsay-Abaire, Billy Bob Thornton, Linda Rae Pierce, Rabbi Chaim Stern, Rabbi Rick Rheins, Mary Wisniewski, Eckhart Tolle, Dr. Nora Wong, C.S. Lewis, and Ram Dass.

These other beautiful people:

Our dear friends, Shining Light Parents, and family who so generously and courageously shared their amazing stories and their loved ones with us: Conrad and Paola Leslie, Christopher Ramirez, Kerry and Denny Cline, Carrie Ann Sill, Nika Sill Morse and the late Hugh Sill, Cathie and Bill Canepa, Linda and Rich Kwasny, John Morehouse, Ainsley Nies, Jeffery Vernon Pehrson, and Jeff Phair.

And my other fraternity brothers- and sorority sisters-in-loss for your valuable contributions to this book and the choices you've made: Patti Reis, Richard Page, Greg and Missy Post, Jeffrey and Anita Miller, John and Alison Barry, Richard Hobbs, and Gary and Kay Weiss.

To all of my beta readers who previewed the manuscript and made it infinitely better, including these dear friends: Lauren Hopkins Winslow, Debbie Weiner, Charlie Myers, and Kim Higgins.

My brother and sister, Grover Gauntt and Laura Butie, for your everlasting love and support and for always being there for us.

Brittany and Ryan Kirby, the most valuable and indispensable players of Team Healing, for your love, insight, and intuition, and bringing joy into our lives.

Our grandsons, Wyatt and Hunter Kirby, and our granddaughter waiting to be born. Thank you for showing us the force of new life is beautiful and strong.

John Dale and Evan Nicholas. Thank you for honoring Jimmy with your love and friendship.

To Professor David Roman and the entire Department of English at the University of Southern California for continuing to honor the memory and legacy of Jimmy Gauntt with the Jimmy Gauntt Memorial Awards, now in its 11th year.

To all of our loved ones on the other side who have touched us and taught us *they've gone away in order to be with us in a new way, even closer than before,* this book is dedicated to you: Rogelio and Christian Ramirez, Hugh and George Sill, Nicolas Leslie, Alex Page, Amanda Post, Ian "Poods" Barry, Ariana Miller, David and Karen Reis, Riley and David Cline, John and Ben, Erica Louise Abbott, Jon Schroeder, Horace Hahn, Jeff Morehouse, Remy Blystone, Sean Canepa, Father Patrick O'Malley, Tom O'Malley, Rhianna Kinglet Dickson Hobbs, Brent MacNab, Bill and Brian Driscoll, Kevin Matthew Kirby, Andie Kwasny, Melissa Loban, Carly Vouvalides, Morgan Boisson, Anna Louise Gauntt, Vernon and Henrietta Case, Joan Westlund Case, Morgan Case, Mary Sawyers Swan Cook, Jimmy Thornton, Danny Hiser, Jana Hagestad, Michael Weiss, Adam Weiner, James W. Tedrow, Banning "Brud" Lary, Brett Lary, Richard Albert Nies, Conchita Zapata, Rev. Thomas Hinkin, James

P. Walton, Joan Kazmarek, Rabbi Chaim Stern, Daniel Wong, David Phair, James Schwark, Victor Pei, and III.

James Tedrow Gauntt and Grover Cleveland Gauntt Jr., my son, my father. Thank you, Jimmy and Dad, for your eternal love and guidance, and showing us it's not a dream—the veil is coming down and we can always "have a catch" with those we deeply love.

Hilary Woodhouse Tedrow Gauntt, my first angel, best friend, the most amazing mother and grandmother a child could ever have, and beloved wife of over 47 years. You are the sun, the moon, the heaven and the stars and everything that is good. You are the most beautiful person I know.

Books Mentioned:
A to Z Healing Toolbox, Susan Hannifin-MacNab
All the Light We Cannot See, Anthony Doerr
Permission to Mourn, Tom Zuba
Messages, Bonnie McEneaney
Rabbit Hole, David Lindsay-Abaire
Companioning the Bereaved, Dr. Alan Wolfelt
The Book of Awakening, Mark Nepo
Man's Search for Meaning, Viktor E. Frankl
Suffering Is the Only Honest Work, Casey and Jimmy Gauntt

Websites/Organizations Mentioned:
Rabbi Regina Sandler-Phillips and Ways of Peace: waysofpeace.org
Helping Parents Heal: www.helpingparentsheal.org
Suzanne Giesemann and Messages of Hope: www.suzannegiesemann.com/radio/
Chris Lynn: www.bluejeanmystic.com
Survivors of Suicide: www.survivorsofsuicide.com
Loloma Foundation: www.lolomafoundation.org
Soaring Spirits International: https://soaringspirits.org

Write Me Something Beautiful: www.writemesomethingbeautiful.
com
Genealogy Bank: www.genealogybank.com
Damonza: https://DamonZa.com
Heron Earth: www.heronearth.com
Just In Time: https://jitfosteryouth.org

Made in the USA
Columbia, SC
21 March 2021